CHINA
in Pictures

Alison Behnke

Lerner Publications Company

Contents

Website address: www.lernerbooks.com

Lerner Publications Company
A division of Lerner Publishing Group
241 First Avenue North
Minneapolis, MN 55401 U.S.A.

web enhanced @ www.vgsbooks.com

Library of Congress Cataloging-in-Publication Data

Behnke, Alison.
        China in pictures / Alison Behnke— Rev. and expanded.
            p.   cm. — (Visual geography series)
        Includes bibliographic references and index.
        Summary: Text and illustrations present detailed information on the geography, history and government, economy, people, cultural life and society of traditional and modern China, home to over one-fifth of the earth's population.
        ISBN: 0-8225-0370-0 (lib. bdg. : alk. paper)
        1. China—Juvenile literature. 2. China—Pictorial works—Juvenile literature. [1. China.] I. Title. II. Visual geography series (Minneapolis, Minn.)
DS712 .B4324 2003
951—dc21   2001007217

Manufactured in the United States of America
1 2 3 4 5 6 - JR - 08 07 06 05 04 03

INTRODUCTION

China—officially called the People's Republic of China, or PRC—spreads across the eastern half of the Asian continent to the sea. The country's landscape ranges from fertile plains to arid deserts. Snowy peaks, wide rivers, rocky plateaus, and terraced hillsides are home to more than fifty ethnic minorities and more than 1 billion people, making China the most populous nation in the world.

China is a country of vast resources and vast needs, and its long history is as full of contradictions as its terrain is full of variety. More than three thousand years ago, powerful emperors controlled an enormous Chinese empire from lavish courts. Ancient China's scientists and scholars invented technological breakthroughs that included paper, movable type, gunpowder, and the magnetic compass. Its authors composed classic poems, novels, and philosophical works, and its artists created beautiful pottery, paintings, and sculpture. But China's peace and prosperity were marred by frequent wars and natural disasters. Power was difficult to hold, and control of the country was hard won

and easily lost. Floods, droughts, and earthquakes struck the nation, shaking its stability with stunning swiftness.

Rebellion and civil war in the early twentieth century ended China's long tradition of monarchy. In 1949 a new era began with the establishment of the People's Republic of China, a Communist government headed by the charismatic leader Mao Zedong (Mao Tse-tung). Mao's ambitious plans to modernize China—from its economy to its ideals—made some progress, but they also brought great hardship to the Chinese population. After Mao's death, Communism remained, but the system and the nation gradually started to move in a new direction.

For many years, China had avoided contact with other countries, but in the late 1900s the government began to develop a new openness to the outside world. Mao's successor, Deng Xiaoping, implemented many economic reforms in the hope of spurring China's growth and improving living conditions for the Chinese people. Communication

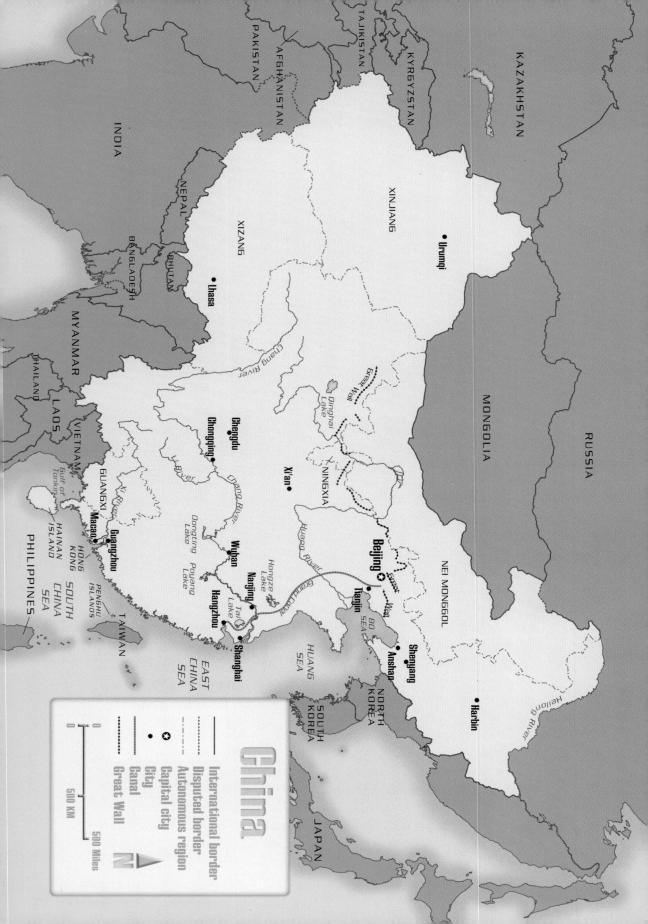

and cooperation between China and foreign countries increased. After Deng's death in 1997, the nation continued to develop and change under the leadership of Jiang Zemin. China joined the World Trade Organization (WTO) in late 2001, marking a significant step toward becoming an even more active member of the international economic and political community.

Modern China is a diverse and complex nation. Chinese leaders still have to deal with serious issues including rural poverty, human rights violations, and AIDS. Yet, even as China faces tremendous challenges, it looks ahead toward great opportunities. The country's task in the twenty-first century will be to reconcile new ideas and influences with its own long-standing beliefs and traditions and to use the lessons of its remarkable but troubled past to create a bright and prosperous future.

PINYIN

The adoption of pinyin, a system for converting Chinese characters into the Latin alphabet, has changed the written form of many Chinese proper names. This list contains some of the most common terms and their pinyin equivalents.

COMMON TERM	PINYIN EQUIVALENT
Geographical Names	
Canton	Guangzhou
Chungking	Chongqing
Gobi Desert	Gebi Desert
Inner Mongolia	Nei Monggol
North China Plain	Huabei Plain
Peking	Beijing
Pescadores	Penghu Islands
Plateau of Tibet	Plateau of Qing Zang
Szechwan	Sichuan
Tibet	Xizang
Yangzi River	Chang River
Yellow River	Huang River
Historical Names	
Chiang Kai-shek	Jiang Jieshi
Ch'in dynasty	Qin dynasty
Ch'ing dynasty	Qing dynasty
Chou dynasty	Zhou dynasty
Chou Enlai	Zhou Enlai
Hsia dynasty	Xia dynasty
Kuomintang	Guomindang
Mao Tse-tung	Mao Zedong
Sung dynasty	Song dynasty
Sun Yat-sen	Sun Zhongshan

THE LAND

China is one of the largest countries in the world, exceeded in size only by Russia and Canada. With about 3.7 million square miles (9,583,000 square kilometers) of territory, China is almost as big as the entire continent of Europe. Its 1.27 billion people make up more than one-fifth of the earth's human inhabitants.

Russia, the largest of China's fourteen neighbors, borders China to the north. Along part of this border, Mongolia nestles between China and Russia. To the northwest are Kazakhstan, Kyrgyzstan, and Tajikistan, all former republics of the Soviet Union. Afghanistan, Pakistan, and India lie to the west and southwest. Natural barriers, such as mountain ranges and thick forests, separate China from Nepal, Bhutan, Myanmar (formerly Burma), Laos, and Vietnam in the south. To the east and southeast are the South China, East China, and Huang (Yellow) Seas, which are arms of the Pacific Ocean. Northeastern China has a short border with North Korea.

China's coastline stretches for more than 8,000 miles (12,874 km).

Many islands lie offshore, including the large island of Taiwan, which since 1950 has been the home of the Nationalist Chinese government. This group ruled mainland China between 1927 and 1949 and continued to regard itself as the rightful government of mainland China after the Communist Party took control. Negotiations regarding unification between Taiwan and the PRC are under way, but results may be a long way off.

Topography

China has one of the world's most diverse landscapes. Within the nation's vast area lie barren deserts, snowcapped mountains, and fertile coastal areas, creating a unique landscape that can be both beautiful and harsh.

Much of western China is desert. The autonomous region of Nei Monggol, also called Inner Mongolia, borders the Gebi (Gobi) Desert in the north and includes the Mu Us Desert in the southwest.

THE GREAT WALL AND THE GRAND CANAL

Two of the Chinese landscape's most impressive features were actually built by humans. The Great Wall has stood for more than 2,500 years. Begun in about the fifth century B.C. and enlarged in later periods, this high stone-and-earth wall may once have extended for more than 6,000 miles (9,656 km), from the Bo Sea in the northeast to Gansu province in the northwest. Vandalism, erosion, and time have reduced the wall's length, but parts of it have been restored.

The Grand Canal—the world's longest artificial waterway—connects the Chang and Huang Rivers. Begun more than two thousand years ago and greatly expanded in the A.D. 600s, the canal stretches between Beijing and Hangzhou, a distance of more than 1,000 miles (1,609 km). Parts of the Grand Canal continue to be used for shipping and transportation.

For links to pictures and more information on the Great Wall, go to vgsbooks.com.

Northwestern China, including the Tarim Basin, the Turpan Depression, and the vast Taklimakan Desert, is also extremely dry.

In addition to its wide deserts, China has steep mountains. In western China, the main ranges are the Tian, the Pamir, and the Himalaya Mountains. The peaks in these ranges are among the highest in the world. China shares the Tian Mountains with Kyrgyzstan. On the border between the two nations lies the range's highest point, Pobeda Peak, at an elevation of 24,406 feet (7,439 meters) above sea level. The Pamirs stretch into several neighboring countries, and this western chain includes many peaks that are over 20,000 feet (6,096 m) high.

The Himalaya Mountains—the tallest range in the world—extend for 1,500 miles (2,414 km) between Pakistan and northeastern India. China's southern frontier includes a large portion of the Himalayas. Mount Everest is the earth's highest point at 29,035 feet (8,850 m) and lies along the border with Nepal. The tallest Himalayan mountain completely within China is Gurla Mandhata (25,355 ft. or 7,728 m).

The Kunlun Mountains run from west to east in the center of China along the northern border of Xizang (Tibet). Many ranges fan out from this chain, the highest peak of which is Ulugh Muztagh, at 25,338 feet (7,723 m) above sea level. In the northeastern corner of China lie the Da Hinggan and Xiao Hinggan Mountains.

China's eastern coast is a landscape of wide plains and plateaus.

The Dongbei (Manchurian) Plain in northeastern China sweeps down to the Huabei (North China) Plain in the central coastal area, one of China's most productive wheat-growing regions. Southeastern China is known for its rice fields as well as for its tall limestone formations.

The Plateau of Tibet—sometimes called the Plateau of Qing Zang—is a striking feature of China's topography. At an altitude of about 15,000 feet (4,572 m), this tableland is the highest in the world. The Kunlun Mountains border the plateau on the north, and the Pamirs lie to the west. Bounded on the south by the Himalayas, the plateau includes most of the autonomous region of Xizang. Two of the nation's main rivers, the Huang (Yellow) and the Chang (Yangzi), begin in the highlands of the plateau. Much of the Plateau of Tibet's terrain is barren, making traditional occupations of farming and herding difficult to practice.

Rivers and Lakes

All of China's major rivers flow eastward toward the Pacific Ocean, keeping the nation's fertile coastal regions well watered. Not surprisingly, most of the country's population live in the east.

China's northernmost waterway is the Heilong River. Over its length of more than 2,000 miles (3,219 km), this river separates eastern China from Russia. During the 1960s, a border dispute flared

The **Chang River** winds its way eastward across China and empties into the East China Sea near Shanghai.

between the two nations for control of the waterway, and parts of the boundary in the northeast are still unsettled.

The 2,903-mile-long (4,672 km) Huang River rises in the mountains of the north central province of Qinghai. The waterway flows parallel to the mountains until it makes a wide sweep northeastward into Nei Monggol. The river eventually turns south and finally travels eastward into the Bo and Huang Seas. The Huang River and its tributaries water expanses of farmland in northern China.

The Huang carries vast quantities of a fine, yellow soil called loess. These deposits have gradually raised the riverbed of the Huang higher over the centuries. As a result, less water can be held within the river's banks, and frequent floods occur when the water overflows.

China's longest waterway is the 3,434-mile-long (5,526 km) Chang River, which feeds a vast network of irrigation ditches, providing water for northern wheat fields and southern rice acreages. The Chang River, like the Huang, originates in the province of Qinghai. The waterway flows in a torrent for hundreds of miles through canyons that it has cut into the mountains. Eventually, the river empties into the East China Sea, north of the important port city of Shanghai.

The Xi River of Guangdong province flows for 1,200 miles (1,931 km) in southeastern China and is largely a commercial sea-lane. Large boats can navigate the Xi as far as the city of Wuzhou, and smaller crafts can travel even farther. The Zhu (Pearl) River forms part of the

Chinese sailors navigate the Li River in a small sampan (flat-bottomed boat).

Xi delta and passes through the city of Guangzhou (Canton).

River-fed lakes dot China's landscape. Among the largest is Dongting Lake, a shallow body of water in Hunan province. When the lake is full of water, it can cover as many as 4,000 square miles (10,360 sq. km). Poyang Lake in Jiangxi province is 90 miles (145 km) long and 20 miles (32 km) wide, and many rivers in southeastern China flow into this body of water. Other important lakes include Tai and Hongze Lakes in eastern China and Qinghai Lake in central China.

Over the centuries, the Huang River has flooded so many times and has caused so much devastation that it is called China's Sorrow. Dikes built along the river have helped somewhat. However, they were temporarily rendered useless in 1938, when Chinese troops intentionally bombed them, hoping that the ensuing flood would defeat advancing Japanese forces.

Climate

Many regional climatic variations exist in China, chiefly because of the nation's huge size and varying altitude. The Plateau of Tibet and parts of northern China experience great extremes in temperature. In the winter, temperatures may drop well below 0°F (–18°C), while summer temperatures in these areas range between 60° and 85°F (16° and 29°C).

The provinces of central China have a milder climate, with average temperatures of 80°F (27°C) in summer and 30°F (–1°C) in winter. The eastern parts of the great basins of the Huang and Chang Rivers experience wet, hot summers and dry, cool winters. The deserts see highs of more than 100°F (38°C) in summer and lows of about 15°F (–9°C) in winter.

Most of China's rain falls between the months of May and October. Monsoons (seasonal winds) bring 20 to 40 inches (51 to 102 centimeters) of annual rain to northeastern China, and southeastern regions get 80 to 120 inches (203 to 305 cm) per year. The deserts and the Plateau of Tibet receive the smallest amounts of precipitation—usually between 4 and 10 inches (10 and 25 cm) annually.

If you'd like to learn what the weather is like in various parts of China right now, visit vgsbooks.com for a link to the most up-to-date weather statistics.

Because the summer rainy season in northwestern China is short, this region is dry nearly all the time. In some southern provinces, rain falls throughout the year, occasionally in amounts that can cause flooding near river basins. Coastal provinces also experience typhoons (violent hurricanes) that can destroy urban centers as well as farmland.

The cities of Chongqing, Wuhan, and Nanjing in south central China have such hot climates that they are known as "the three furnaces." China's lowest point, the Turpan Depression, is also a hot area, reaching temperatures of over 100°F (38°C) in the summer.

▷ Flora and Fauna

Hundreds of years of intense farming and urban expansion have destroyed much of China's original vegetation. Only in remote mountain areas do natural forests survive, including stands of oaks, maples, larches, and birches. Rain forests exist south of the Chang River and contain a mixture of evergreens and palms.

Southern China features a variety of subtropical species, including bamboo trees, ginkgos (trees with fan-shaped leaves and yellow fruit), laurels, and magnolias. Western China hosts drought-resistant grasses, herbs, and desert scrub. Vegetation is somewhat more plentiful in the southwest and includes alpine grasses and mountain flowers.

Bamboo, a type of giant grass, is native to China. The bamboo stem can be used to make fishing poles, tools, and cooking utensils, and the leaves make a tasty meal for hungry pandas.

With fewer than one thousand **giant pandas** left in the wild, the giant panda has become a symbol of Chinese wildlife and of endangered animals everywhere. To learn more about giant pandas, visit vgsbooks. com for links to websites with in-depth information and photographs.

The forests bordering Xizang and Sichuan (Szechwan) are the home of the bamboo-eating giant panda. In Xizang, the goat, yak (a relative of the ox), and dzo (a cross between a yak and a cow) are native animals. These creatures also share their habitat with the takin (goat antelope) and the musk deer.

Two-humped Bactrian camels live in Xinjiang, and water buffalo are valued in southern China as work animals. The tropical regions of the nation are home to primates such as macaques and gibbons. Hooved animals such as gazelles, deer, and antelope thrive in herds in the western uplands.

Alligators inhabit the rivers of east central China, and four-foot-long (1.2 m) salamanders slither in and out of the waterways of western China. The nation's bird population includes peacocks, herons, and cranes.

Although China is still home to a wealth of wildlife, pollution, loss of habitat, and other factors threaten many native species. Only a few tigers and bears still roam the country, and the snow leopard of western China is endangered. The *baiji,* a river dolphin, was once common in the Chang River, but pollution and overcrowding have severely reduced its numbers. Organizations inside and outside of China are working to protect these and other animals.

Natural Resources and the Environment

China has a large variety of mineral resources. Its deposits of antimony (used in alloys) and tungsten (a hard, heat-resistant mineral) are the world's largest. The nation's reserves of tin, aluminum, copper, zinc, and lead are also abundant.

Extensive amounts of coal exist in the central provinces of Shaanxi, Guizhou, and Sichuan, as well as in the northern part of Xinjiang and in the eastern province of Shandong. Because of such plentiful coal reserves, the Chinese government has been slow to switch from steam locomotives for its railways to more efficient diesel engines or electric trains.

Petroleum mining and exploration take place off China's eastern coast and in the southern provinces. The main oil fields of western China are in Xinjiang, near the city of Urumqi. More recent sites have opened in northeastern China, and offshore drilling platforms are located in the South China Sea, the Gulf of Tonkin, and the Bo Sea (also called Bo Hai).

Although its vast amount of land is one of China's greatest natural resources, the country's huge population puts a great strain on its environment. Natural disasters such as droughts and floods pose additional challenges. Desertification—the transformation of arable land into desert—is a major problem, especially in northern and western

GORGEOUS GORGES

China's energy needs and water problems led the government to begin construction on a massive dam on the Chang River in 1994. Scheduled for completion by 2009, the Three Gorges Dam is named for a dramatic series of hills and mountains that slope down to the waterway. If successful, the dam, with its huge reservoir and system of locks, would provide hydroelectric power, improve shipping and transportation capabilities, and ease flooding. However, it will raise the river's water level so high that the gorges will be almost completely submerged, along with farmland and historical sites. More than one million people will be relocated. Environmentalists worry about the possible effects on the river's ecosystem, and many people mourn the loss of such beautiful and unique scenery.

China. Pollution troubles many of the nation's cities and waterways, and deforestation and erosion are ongoing environmental issues.

Cities

More than one-fourth of China's people live in urban areas. The nation's three largest cities—Shanghai, Beijing (Peking), and Tianjin—are not part of any province or state. Instead, each one is a separate municipality that reports directly to the central government. Chongqing (Chungking) was recently made a fourth municipality.

Crowded Shanghai, with more than 13 million people, is the most populous urban center in China. China's primary commercial center, Shanghai is also one of the nation's most important port cities and handles much of the country's domestic and foreign trade.

Beijing (population more than 11 million) is the capital of China. Lying in the northeastern part of the country, the city contains some of the nation's most important monuments and historical treasures. Expansion and industrialization have changed the face of Beijing in recent decades, and thousands of buses and several freeways transport people and goods throughout the capital. Beijing's colorful markets offer fruits, vegetables, meats, and consumer goods from the farms and factories of surrounding regions. Colleges and universities are scattered throughout the capital.

Shanghai, which is located in eastern China near the East China Sea, is an important port city. During the 1990s, Shanghai grew rapidly, adding thousands of residential and commercial buildings and a subway system.

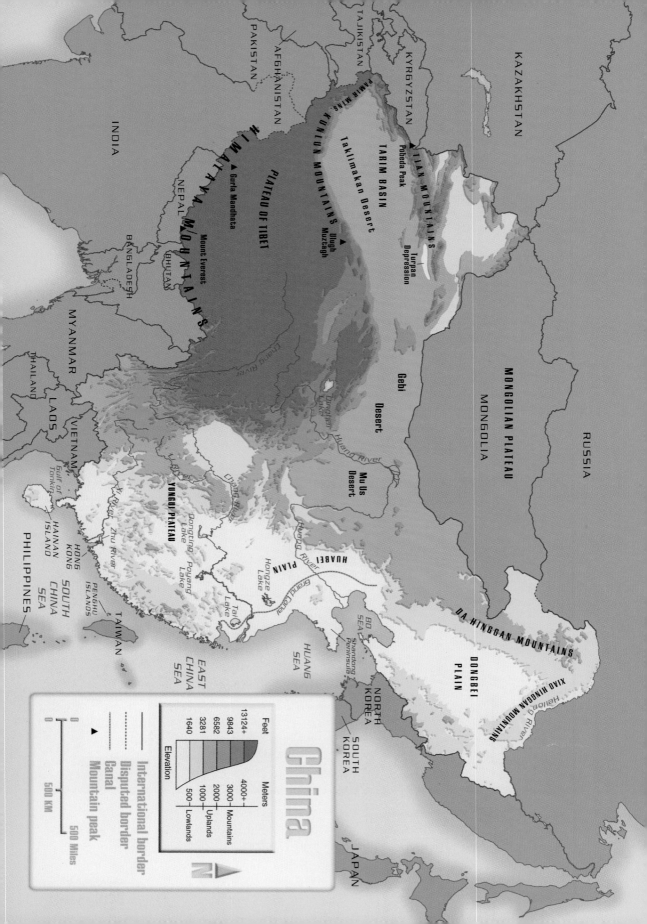

As China's capital, Beijing was once home to the country's emperors and their families, who lived in the royal complex called **the Forbidden City.**

Located near the Bo Sea, Tianjin (population more than 9 million) is a major transportation hub and industrial center. Large ships can berth in the city's harbor, and local factories produce goods including automobiles, elevators, sewing machines, and cameras.

Guangzhou (population more than 4 million) is the capital of Guangdong province and an important center for international trade. In addition to products from surrounding farms, the city offers factory-made items such as cement, steel, chemicals, and fertilizers for sale in its markets and stores. Zhongshan University, noted for its medical school, is among many colleges and other institutions located in Guangzhou.

More than 3 million people live in the city of Chongqing, at the junction of the Jialing and Chang Rivers. Chongqing municipality, formed in 1997, has a total of more than 30 million residents. Workers on recent expansion projects have renovated Chongqing's streets, have constructed parks, and have improved urban transportation. The city's broad manufacturing base includes the making of tools, machinery, chemicals, and textiles.

Other major cities in China include Chengdu, Nanjing (Nanking), Shenyang, Wuhan, Urumqi, and Harbin. China also includes the two special administrative regions (SARs) of Hong Kong and Macao, once outposts of European power. Hong Kong (population 6.9 million) became a British colony in the 1800s and was returned to Chinese control in 1997. Macao, with a population of more than 400,000, was claimed as a trading center in 1557 by the Portuguese and remained under Portugal's power until it was restored to Chinese authority in 1999.

HISTORY AND GOVERNMENT

China has one of the oldest written histories in the world, but the earliest records of Chinese settlement are archaeological. Bones, pottery, and other artifacts indicate that the predecessors of modern humans inhabited China more than 1.3 million years ago. From these early ancestors developed the Stone Age peoples of the Yangshao and the Longshan cultures.

The Yangshao culture flourished in the valley of the Huang River between 5000 B.C. and 3000 B.C. Its people probably hunted, fished, and farmed. The Longshan group also farmed, cultivating rice and raising livestock. The Longshan may have developed from and displaced the Yangshao, or the two cultures may have arisen separately during the same time period and come into contact with each other later.

According to folklore, the Xia dynasty (family of rulers) followed the Yangshao and Longshan cultures. Although no archaeological evidence supports its existence, the Xia period persists in Chinese legend.

▶ Early Recorded History

The first Chinese administration for which written records exist is the Shang dynasty. Governing a largely agricultural society, the Shang dynasty controlled north central China between the eighteenth and twelfth centuries B.C.

The Zhou people from western China attacked and defeated the Shang dynasty in the twelfth or eleventh century B.C. The Zhou dynasty lasted for almost nine hundred years and divided China into small kingdoms that belonged to individual warlords (local military leaders) with close ties to the dynasty's ruler. This subdivision of power eventually led to internal warfare, and Zhou rule ended in 221 B.C., when Qin Shi Huangdi—head of a strong, well-organized realm—defeated the warlords and established his capital near Xi'an.

Qin Shi Huangdi is regarded as China's first emperor. Although he had a reputation as a cruel leader who put many of his subjects to death, his reign also saw many advances. During the Qin dynasty, farming, livestock raising, and silk making were common livelihoods. Workers built dams and canals, and a series of thick, high walls—which the Zhou dynasty had built to keep out nomadic peoples of Mongolia—were connected and extended to form part of the Great Wall. The realm had an advanced trading economy, and scholars skilled in poetry, philosophy, music, and painting recorded historical events.

The Qin empire stretched from the foothills of the Mongolian Plateau in the north to the basin of the Chang River in the south. The emperor's armies also advanced farther south into the coastal areas near Guangzhou and conquered what would later become northern Vietnam. The Qin dynasty established imperial unity, enabling the successive Han dynasty to rule for four centuries.

Han Dynasty

During the Han dynasty (206 B.C. to A.D. 220), China made further economic and cultural advances. Han rulers introduced the manufacture of paper to Korea, Japan, India, and the Arabian Peninsula. Scientists invented the seismograph to record earthquakes and made great advances in astronomy. Chinese craftspeople produced fine-quality porcelain, silk brocades, and strong wool. Envoys sent to the borderlands of the west met traders from India and Persia (modern Iran) and established the Silk Road, a trade route between China and countries to its west. The Spice Route, another important trade route, brought China into commercial contact with Southeast Asia.

Despite its decades of achievement, the last century of Han rule was unstable. Corruption, rivalry, and rebellion plagued the state, and the dynasty ended in disorder in A.D. 220. Three kingdoms—the Wei, the Shu, and the Wu—eventu-

Camel caravans of merchants traveled the Silk Road to trade Chinese goods in lands to the west.

ally emerged but shared power for only a few decades. The rival king-doms gave way to a period of splintered rule and more than three hundred years of disunity. The Sui dynasty finally reunited China in the sixth century A.D. During the reign of the Sui family, the emperor Sui Wendi constructed the Grand Canal, one of the world's outstanding engineering achievements. Peasant rebellions and natu-ral disasters weakened the Sui dynasty, and a rival group—the Tang—took power in the seventh century.

Tang and Song Dynasties

Between the seventh and ninth centuries, the Tang dynasty saw many developments. Rulers of the dynasty began to select members of the civil service by examination, and governments from present-day North and South Korea and Xizang recognized Chinese authority. Trade extended along the Silk Road to Samarqand (in present-day Uzbekistan) and Constantinople (in modern Turkey) and went by sea to regions near the Persian Gulf.

The peak years of achievement were followed by a rebellion in the mid-eighth century and gradual decline during the ninth century. Heavy taxation, forced labor, obligatory military service, palace

This relief is one of many **Tang dynasty artworks** depicting horses. Tang leaders greatly increased the number and the quality of China's horses by importing new breeds and developing new ways to care for the animals.

extravagance, and bureaucratic corruption once more weakened the empire. These problems allowed other groups to seize power.

For more than a century, conflict and division disrupted China. But in 960, Song Taizu took power and established the Song dynasty, which reunited the empire under a strong central government. During the three hundred years of Song rule, trade expansion, urban growth, and technical progress continued. Improvements in navigation brought greater maritime (seafaring) trade, and Korean, Persian, and Arab commercial communities developed in the ports of Guangzhou and Hangzhou. The government expanded mining, ship-building, and silk making and introduced paper currency throughout the empire. Gunpowder and movable type were also invented.

During the Song dynasty, another innovation—paper currency—came into wide use in China. Accustomed to carrying heavy metal coins, Chinese shoppers and businesspeople nicknamed the new bills "flying money" or "flying cash" because they were so light that a breeze could carry them away.

In the twelfth century, a nomadic group attacked the northern Song holdings, forcing the Song court to move south. The disrupted empire split into two parts and was ruled by Northern and Southern Song dynasties. A familiar pattern repeated itself when court corruption and rural discontent made both dynasties ripe for overthrow by a new threat from the north—the Mongols.

Mongol and Ming Rule

A nomadic people from Mongolia, the Mongols were skilled horse riders and archers. In 1206 they had been united under the Yuan dynasty, headed by Genghis Khan. (A khan was a ruler of the Mongol people.) By 1215 Genghis and his troops had captured Beijing and were pushing westward to southern Russia. By 1234 the Mongols had occupied Northern Song holdings, and in 1279 the last Southern Song possessions fell to Genghis's grandson Kublai Khan.

Kublai Khan ruled an extended empire, which stretched from eastern China to the Caspian Sea. Under the Yuan dynasty—the first foreign group to rule all of China—trade and crafts flourished, and engineers improved and extended the Grand Canal. Yet, despite its wealth and prestige, the empire was too vast to remain united. After Kublai Khan's death in 1294, the empire's subregions, called khanates, fought against one another. This rivalry weakened the Yuan dynasty, allowing Zhu Yuanzhang, the leader of a secret society called the Red Turbans, to seize Nanjing in 1356. By 1368 he had control of the middle and lower reaches of the Chang River, and in that same year he declared himself Ming Taizu—the first ruler of the Ming dynasty.

Between 1368 and 1644, Ming rulers governed a stable and prosperous empire. Ming Taizu's successors moved the court to Beijing, and royal builders constructed many palaces and temples in and around the city. In addition, the government repaired the crumbling Great Wall and established trade and diplomatic relations with more than thirty countries. Ming historians recorded the visits of dignitaries from as far away as Italy and the Netherlands, and representatives of the Ming court traveled to countries in Asia and Africa. Visitors to China included Roman Catholic missionaries. Most missionaries failed to attract much local interest, although the priest Matteo Ricci established a moderate following. Many Chinese distrusted European diplomats and merchants.

During the Ming dynasty, Chinese society also became more developed. Royalty had always existed at the top of the system, and poor farmers, or peasants, had always been at the bottom. With expanded trade, education, and access to books, the middle classes broadened and grew, from merchants and artisans to scholars and landowners.

Despite its strengths, the Ming dynasty experienced constant border disputes, particularly with the Mongols and the Japanese. Internal unrest also occurred during the seventeenth century, when famine and poverty led to popular uprisings against the regime. Rebel troops under the leadership of a rural

THE ROAD TO CATHAY

Marco Polo, an explorer from Venice, Italy, traveled to China in the late 1200s and spent close to twenty years there. The explorer's vivid accounts of Kublai Khan's fabulous palaces, gardens, and pavilions astounded the courts of Europe and spurred commercial interest in China. Soon European traders and ambassadors set out for the region that Polo had called Cathay.

Marco Polo

worker named Li Zicheng marched on Beijing in 1644, briefly capturing the city. Manchurian troops, which had overthrown Ming power in the northeast beyond China's boundary, forced Li to retreat. The Manchu set up the Qing dynasty, and another foreign power ruled Chinese territory.

Qing Dynasty and Trade with Europe

Unlike previous foreign rulers, the Manchu adopted much of Chinese culture and government. As a result, the Qing dynasty enjoyed stability and expanded its territory. The population increased, and livelihoods such as agriculture and handicrafts experienced rapid expansion.

Although foreigners had traditionally been unwelcome, the Manchu established an official market in Guangzhou for foreign trade. However, tight restrictions governed commerce with the outside world—a situation that Great Britain, a major European trading power, found unacceptable. In 1793 the British sent a messenger to the Qianlong emperor to request the opening of a British embassy in Beijing, along with greater trading freedoms. The Chinese refused.

By the end of the eighteenth century, Qing prosperity had declined,

and political corruption was rampant. Anti-Qing rebellions among the common people greatly weakened the regime, giving European powers the opportunity to assert themselves in the nineteenth century.

The British were concerned that the Chinese did not want to buy British goods. The traders offered European items in exchange for Chinese tea, silk, and porcelain. However, because the money that the British spent to buy China's goods was much more than they earned from the sale of British commodities, Britain faced a serious trade imbalance. British merchants resorted to exchanging the addictive drug opium, instead of British goods, for Chinese products.

The Chinese government became alarmed by the growing addiction of its people to opium and by the outflow of silver to pay for the drug. The Qing administration appointed a special commissioner to find a solution. After negotiations with the British failed to stop the opium trade, the commissioner publicly destroyed thousands of chests of opium that had been seized from British merchants. The British retaliated, and the first Opium War erupted in 1839. The conflict lasted until the British defeated the Chinese in 1842. Under the Treaty of Nanjing, the victorious British imposed many demands on the Chinese regarding trade. Among other concessions, the British took over both the island of Hong Kong and part of the nearby Kowloon Peninsula.

⊙ Rebellion and Reform

The drain on China's silver to pay for opium grew even larger after the Treaty of Nanjing. In addition, severe famines, droughts, and floods afflicted millions of Chinese. The corrupt Qing bureaucracy did little to ease the plight of villagers, and anti-Qing movements arose yet again. The most famous uprising was the Taiping Rebellion, which lasted from 1851 to 1864. Begun in southern China, the revolt soon spread and resulted in the deaths of as many as

The flags of many nations flew over **Guangzhou,** where foreign traders did business with Chinese merchants.

thirty million Chinese. The rebellion's leaders preached the building of a freer, more democratic society. They wanted to abolish social inequalities and to prohibit alcohol use and gambling. The movement's followers occupied Wuhan and established a government at Nanjing, and for more than a decade the rebels ruled nearly half of China.

After a second opium war in the 1850s, foreign powers had gained concessions from the Qing leaders. These new privileges included the legalization of the opium trade and the opening of more ports for foreign commerce. To foreigners, the rebellious Taiping government was in the way of progress. It had banned opium and had restricted the freedom of foreigners in important centers such as Shanghai. These international powers wanted to help the Manchu eliminate the rebels. After a lengthy siege, Nanjing fell in 1864, and the conflict ended.

After the Taiping Rebellion was finally put down, the Manchu became aware of the need for change. They enacted agricultural and industrial reforms and extended educational opportunities. But these internal measures did not solve growing international troubles. Foreign powers demanded more trade concessions and also began to take over Chinese territory. The French absorbed the region that would become Vietnam, and the British enlarged Hong Kong and

Even after the Chinese government outlawed the **opium trade,** smugglers continued to exchange silk, porcelain, and other Chinese goods for the addictive drug.

During **the Boxer Uprising**, American, British, and Japanese troops storm Beijing.

seized present-day Myanmar. Following the Chinese-Japanese War in 1894 and 1895, the Japanese took territory in Korea as well as the island of Taiwan and the Penghu Islands (Pescadores).

Manchu intellectuals demanded more reforms to strengthen the nation. However, before any reforms were implemented, another internal group acted against the outsiders. The Yihequan was an anti-Christian, antiforeign secret society that Europeans called the Boxers. In 1900 the Boxer Uprising erupted, resulting in the deaths of many Christians, in the sieges of foreign outposts, and in the destruction of much of northern China. Troops from European nations arrived to put down the uprising. After the defeat of the Boxers, these foreign countries imposed further economic demands on the Manchu.

⊙ Republic of China

Anti-imperial groups flourished in China during the early twentieth century. In 1905 Sun Zhongshan (Sun Yat-sen) founded the Revolutionary Alliance. His organization was dedicated to four goals: driving out the Manchu rulers; restoring China as its own nation; establishing a democratic republic; and distributing landownership more equally. Sun's rebel movement gained momentum between 1905 and 1911 and staged many attacks on Qing power. In October 1911,

Sun Zhongshan

imperial army troops revolted against the government, winning widespread support for the Revolutionary Alliance. In January 1912, the Republic of China was established in Nanjing with a temporary government and with Sun as president.

Overshadowing Sun's power was Yuan Shikai—the strongest warlord in China. He took over Beijing and forced Puyi, the last Chinese emperor, to resign. To avoid civil war, Sun accepted Yuan as the provisional president of China. As Yuan's power expanded, support for Sun declined. In 1913, after a failed second revolution by forces opposing Yuan's dictatorship, Sun fled to Japan. Yuan, with the help of other warlords, unsuccessfully attempted to establish himself as emperor.

Guomindang and Communist Movements

In the Treaty of Versailles following World War I (1914–1918), China lost some of its territory to Japan. Chinese demonstrations against the land losses occurred on May 4, 1919, and were later called the May Fourth Movement. Sun, back from Japan, took advantage of these antigovernment sentiments to build local support for his new Guomindang (Kuomintang), or Nationalist Party.

Sun also sought international help in forming a Chinese republic. Many Chinese were unhappy with the United States and European nations for their decisions at Versailles. However, a growing number of people were interested in Communism and other political theories being explored in the newly established Soviet Union (formerly Russia). The Soviet government encouraged the spread of these ideas in other countries, and it offered aid to Sun Zhongshan in forming a new system in China. The Soviet Union's Comintern, an organization dedicated to spreading Communism, assisted the growth of the Chinese Communist Party (CCP), formed in 1921. Sun grew convinced that victory over the warlords lay in joining forces with the Communists. Thereafter, the Guomindang admitted Communists to its membership and set up a military academy near Guangzhou. A young officer named Jiang Jieshi (Chiang Kai-shek) became head of the academy.

After Sun Zhongshan's death in 1925, Jiang Jieshi followed him as leader of the Guomindang (the Nationalists). Still working with the

Equipped with modern machine guns, Sun Zhongshan's **Nationalist troops** fought Chinese warlords for control of the provinces in the early 1900s. Go to vgsbooks.com for links where you can learn more about the history of warfare in China.

Communists, Jiang brought southern China under control, established a government at Wuhan, and took Shanghai. Soon afterward, differing political ideals and visions of China's future led Jiang and other members of his party to break with the Communists.

Jiang and the Nationalists staged a coup within the Guomindang and removed the Communists. By 1928 Jiang had established a national government at Nanjing and the CCP administration in Wuhan had nearly collapsed. Within a year, Beijing—the center of warlord activity—was also under the Guomindang's authority. Anticommunist nations in Europe, along with the United States, recognized Jiang's government, giving it international legitimacy.

Despite its weakened position, the CCP did not crumble. It organized a peasant uprising in the province of Hunan, hoping to disrupt the Nationalist government. The rebellion, led by a passionate young villager named Mao Zedong (Mao Tse-tung), fueled public anger against Jiang. The Nationalists and the Communists were ready for conflict.

The Communists attempted to set up a rival government in southern China. Jiang was determined to break their power and numbers. His forces attempted to blockade the Red (Communist) Army, which broke through Jiang's lines in the province of Jiangxi and began a retreat known as the Long March in 1934. The Red Army reached the northern province of Shaanxi in 1935 and established a base there. During the march, CCP members chose Mao Zedong as leader of the party.

Under Mao, the Red Army and the CCP strengthened the Communist movement and dedicated themselves to revolutionary goals that included land reforms and equal rights for women. The Nationalist forces, on the other hand, became known for their corruption and for their poor military training.

Retreating from Nationalist forces, the Red Army set out on the Long March. This exhausting year-long trek covered more than 6,000 miles (9,656 km) of nearly inaccessible mountains and crossed some of China's mightiest rivers. Only a few thousand of the original 100,000 Red Army soldiers survived the journey.

The Communists were not Jiang's only enemies. Throughout the 1930s, the Japanese, seeking land and raw materials, seized territory in northern China and along the coast. At first, Jiang's government was more concerned about the Communists than about the Japanese. However, Jiang feared that the CCP would turn the widespread national anger over Japan's actions against the Nationalist government. In 1936 Jiang's own Nationalist troops arrested him and forced him to sign an alliance with the CCP to jointly evict the invaders, and the second Chinese-Japanese War began in 1937.

World War II and Its Aftermath

When Asia became involved in World War II in 1941, China had been at war with Japan for four years. China joined the Allies against Japan, Italy, and Nazi Germany.

Within China, Communist guerrilla bands in the north actively resisted the Japanese, who had by that time occupied Beijing, Shanghai, Nanjing, and Guangzhou. Jiang accepted U.S. aid during the rest of the war, and after Japan's surrender in 1945, Jiang—with U.S. backing—took over many cities in northern China.

But Jiang and his supporters had underestimated CCP strength, which had grown during the war. They also had not accounted for the appeal of Communist ideas to millions of rural and urban workers. The CCP's propaganda attracted the Chinese masses and left the

An American plane drops ammunition for Chinese troops during World War II.

increasingly unpopular Nationalists in a weakened political position. Neither side felt that it could cooperate with its opponent, and full-scale civil war erupted between the Communists and the Nationalists in mid-1946. By the end of 1948, the Red Army had driven Nationalist forces out of northeastern China. In January 1949, Beijing fell without a struggle.

The People's Liberation Army (PLA), as the Red Army came to be called, forged ahead to the Chang River. By the autumn of 1949, all of China except Xizang had been occupied. On October 1, Mao Zedong declared the formation of the People's Republic of China (PRC) in Beijing. In late 1949, Jiang and some of his supporters fled to Taiwan, where they relocated the Nationalist government.

The People's Republic of China

Under Mao Zedong, old methods of governing China were abolished. Mao's supporter Zhou Enlai had authority over government ministries. During the 1950s, Zhou began to redistribute land and to nationalize (change from private to state ownership) industry and business. Financial support from the Soviet Union bolstered the new regime, which implemented five-year plans to revitalize the Chinese economy.

In 1958 Mao introduced the Great Leap Forward—a set of ideas designed to make China economically self-sufficient. The government expanded industry and manufacturing. Agriculture was organized into communes, a form of group farming. Although most acreages were small, more than twenty thousand people often lived on one commune. Commune workers were organized into small groups, called production brigades, to maximize productivity. The profit motive (working for personal gain) disappeared, and the idea that all labor and wages were equal took the place of individual incentives.

Despite its broad vision of improving China, the Great Leap Forward failed. In fact, it led not only to a decline in industrial output but also to drops in food production, resulting in a famine that starved millions of people between 1958 and 1962.

External and Internal Struggles

Mao Zedong

In the early 1960s, China's relations with the Soviet Union severely deteriorated as Mao became critical of what he saw as the Soviets' weakened commitment to pure Communism. China believed itself to be the guardian of Communist ideals and saw conflict with non-Communist nations as inevitable. In 1960 the Soviet Union stopped sending aid and advisers to China, and in 1962 the Soviets did not support China in its brief border war with India.

In 1966 Mao generated another radical change called the Great Proletarian Cultural Revolution, which was designed to foster and revive pure Communist ideals. The Cultural Revolution was partially the result of one branch of the government, led by Mao, conflicting with another branch of the government, under the control of Liu Shaoqi. Mao distrusted moderate trends emerging in the government, while his opponents—including Liu and Deng Xiaoping—advocated less ideological and more practical approaches to running the country.

Inspired by Mao's ideas, groups of Chinese students called the Red Guards attacked traditional society, as well as individuals who appeared to have Nationalist Party, capitalist,

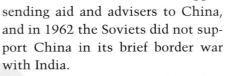

A REGION OF RESISTANCE

In 1950—when the region was still known as Tibet—the Chinese invaded Xizang. The Dalai Lama (Tibet's spiritual leader) and thousands of his followers fled to India, where they established a government in exile. Frequent uprisings occured in Xizang during the 1950s as the Tibetans resisted Chinese rule. Subdued by 1959, the region was claimed by the PRC as part of its territory. In spite of oppresion by the Chinese government, Tibetans continue to practice their religion and culture as far as they are able.

or other anti-Communist ties. Many universities were closed, and Mao urged students to learn from the peasants by living in communes. Red Guards publicly humiliated teachers and skilled managers, and many artists and intellectuals were persecuted. As many as 100 million people died or served time in hard-labor camps during this period of national upheaval.

By the late 1960s, two political views had emerged to deal with China's economic and social problems. Each standpoint was championed by a leader close to Mao. Lin Biao, Mao's presumed successor, favored a closer relationship with the Soviet Union and other Communist or revolutionary nations. Zhou Enlai advocated a more moderate approach, which would include contacts with the United States and Europe.

Lin Biao died in 1971, and support for his political stance weakened. In the same year, the United Nations (UN) recognized the People's Republic of China as the legitimate government of China, and the PRC replaced Taiwan as China's representative in the UN.

China also improved its relations with the United States. In 1972 U.S. president Richard Nixon visited China. Trade, tourism, and diplomatic relations between the two nations slowly developed after the visit. This new cooperation and China's troubled relationship with the Soviet Union signaled the end of the Cultural Revolution. Although Zhou Enlai's view had prevailed, his death in January 1976 left the future of China's leadership uncertain. As Mao aged, he sought a successor among the CCP's members. Although Deng Xiaoping had been

President Richard Nixon and his wife stand on the Great Wall during their visit to China in 1972.

Members of the army denounce Deng Xiaoping in 1976.

favored before Zhou's death, he was disliked by the influential "Gang of Four," made up of Mao's wife and three other radical party members. Without Zhou's support, Deng lost his positions in the government.

After Mao Zedong's death on September 9, 1976, the Gang of Four faced arrest and trial for trying to seize power. Deng returned to the political scene and quickly gained influence, placing his choices of party members in power. By 1980 Deng was effectively China's leader, and he aimed to invigorate the government with young, educated Communists. Many longtime and highly placed supporters of Mao were convicted of corruption and replaced by people from midlevel positions in the party. In addition to these bureaucratic and political changes, economic reforms were important to Deng's government, including the growth of investment and trade with Japan and the United States.

Old and New Issues

Despite China's change in direction, continuing conflicts and new problems surfaced in the late 1980s. Attention again focused on the autonomous region of Xizang. In the late 1980s, Xizang experienced religious unrest in Lhasa, the capital of the autonomous region. In this historic city, demonstrating Buddhist monks clashed with Chinese police. Similar riots erupted in other towns, as groups in Xizang pushed for independence. Discontent over Xizang's status has continued into the twenty-first century.

A new problem in China—student unrest—also became apparent in the late 1980s. In April of 1989, Chinese university students began to demonstrate in favor of democratic reform and the end of political corruption. Their gatherings took place for several weeks in Beijing's Tiananmen Square and became the focus of international interest as the number of protesting students and workers swelled to the hundreds of thousands. In June the government sent troops to the area with orders to end the demonstration. Violence erupted between the soldiers and the protesters, with hundreds killed and thousands wounded in the conflict.

Following the Tiananmen Square incident, power shifted in the Chinese government. By 1990 Deng Xiaoping had retired from all official posts, but major decisions still required his approval. Deng's failing

Approximately 100,000 students and workers calling for freedom and democracy protested in **Tiananmen Square** on May 4, 1989. For links to in-depth coverage of the Tiananmen Square protest, go to vgsbooks.com.

health became a serious concern as government officials vied for leadership of the Communist Party. After Deng's death in February 1997, Jiang Zemin, chosen by Deng as his successor, vowed to continue Deng's economic reforms and policies. Jiang demonstrated his commitment to reform in 2001 with the announcement that private-business owners and capitalists would be allowed to join the CCP.

Other major developments have included the incorporation of the former European colonies of Hong Kong (in 1997) and Macao (in 1999) as special administrative regions of China. These regions are given a high level of autonomy under a policy known as "one country, two systems." The policy's success or failure may influence negotiations regarding the unification of mainland China and Taiwan. Although both China and Taiwan express a wish for peaceful relations, Chinese leaders have also stated that they are willing to use force if necessary.

The Chinese government continued to seek more open relations with the outside world as the twenty-first century began, meeting with leaders and diplomats from world powers such as the United States and Russia. Relations between the United States and China were strained in April of 2001 when a damaged American spy plane was forced to land in China and its crew was detained by Chinese officials. However, open communication had resumed by later that year, and the countries' leaders continue to work together toward policies that will benefit both nations. Within China, as some of its policies became less restrictive, China's pro-democracy movement pressured the government to allow opposition parties and free elections.

Another shift in party power may alter China's direction, as Jiang is scheduled to retire from his position as head of state in 2003. The government's stability and the country's international affairs will depend largely on Jiang's successors and their policies.

Government

The Chinese Constitution identifies the National People's Congress (NPC) as the government's most important legislative organization. The Chinese Communist Party, headed by a party chairman or general secretary, overwhelmingly dominates the membership of the Congress. Since the Congress is too large to be an effective instrument of daily policy and legislation, the smaller Central Committee and its two main bodies, the Politburo and the Standing Committee, exercise power in the name of the Congress.

To handle executive matters, the NPC elects a State Council and its own Standing Committee, consisting of a premier and ministers. Since its members come from the most powerful ranks of the CCP and often hold important posts in the party, the State Council reflects the

China's president **Jiang Zemin** met with U.S. president George W. Bush in Shanghai on October 20, 2001.

party's stance on most issues. The NPC also selects a president and vice president as heads of state. China has begun to experiment with public elections in which the people vote, but most officials are still chosen by the CCP and existing governmental bodies.

The highest judicial power is the Supreme People's Court, which ensures that the CCP's policies are enforced. This court also supervises lower courts at the provincial and local levels.

China is divided into provinces, autonomous regions, municipalities (urban areas), and special administrative regions. The autonomous regions (Xizang, Ningxia, Nei Monggol, Xinjiang, and Guangxi) have some degree of self-rule, especially in the realm of culture. Approximately seventy million members of non-Chinese groups, called national minorities, live in these areas. The self-governing municipalities are Beijing, Shanghai, Tianjin, and Chongqing. Independent administrations run these cities and report directly to the central government. The special administrative regions are Hong Kong and Macao.

THE PEOPLE

Most of China's 1.27 billion inhabitants live in the fertile, eastern one-third of the country. Many urban residents work in factories, shops, or businesses, while most rural inhabitants raise crops or livestock. Throughout China, the standard of living is rising. At the beginning of the twenty-first century, increasing numbers of families could afford to buy televisions, radios, bicycles, refrigerators, computers, cars, and other items that were once considered luxuries.

The position and rights of women have also improved. Before the revolution in 1911, fathers could sell their daughters into marriage or slavery, and husbands could force their wives into prostitution. Modern Chinese women work in government and industry and are members of the armed forces. Nevertheless, women in China still face prejudice, and many skilled women advance more slowly in their professions and receive lower pay than men with similar qualifications and training. As China continues to change and adapt, its people will experience both new benefits and new challenges.

○ National Minorities

About 92 percent of the population is of Mongolian ancestry and is called Han, or ethnic Chinese. In addition to the Han, there are more than fifty other ethnic groups in China. The government recognizes these communities, which together make up only 8 percent of the population, as national minorities. Most of these minorities are concentrated in autonomous regions that were once independent but have been absorbed by China. The groups in these regions often have ethnic ties with peoples in neighboring countries.

The government permits national minorities some cultural independence, and, in some cases, a degree of political self-rule. Most minorities are allowed to study their own language as well as Mandarin Chinese (also called Putongua, the official language of China), to observe traditional religions, and to dress in traditional clothing. In addition, minorities are not subject to the government policy that limits population growth among the Han.

China's 15.6 million Zhuang, most of whom live in Guangxi (a southern autonomous region), are ethnically related to groups in Thailand and constitute the largest national minority. The Hui, with over 8 million members, are Chinese-speaking Muslims (followers of the Islamic religion). They dwell in Ningxia, Gansu, and Qinghai in north central China, and many make their living by herding livestock.

The Turkic-speaking Uygur inhabit the deserts of Xinjiang and have language affiliations with the bordering nations of Kazakhstan, Kyrgyzstan, and Tajikistan. Most members of this group raise animals and cultivate crops near oases (fertile areas that lie within desert regions), and like the Hui, many Uygur are Muslims. Other national minorities include the Yi, the Mongolians, the Miao, and the Kazakhs.

Perhaps the most distinctly non-Chinese minority are the Tibetans, most of whom reside in the highlands of Xizang and in Qinghai (western autonomous regions). They make their livings as farmers and herders. Tibetans follow Lamaism, or Tibetan Buddhism, a religion that is a mixture of traditional Buddhism and local beliefs.

Visit vgsbooks.com for links to websites where you can learn to write Chinese characters and find out more about China's various ethnic groups, including Tibetans.

This **Tibetan couple** lives in Xigazê, Xizang.

Language

Instead of a lettered alphabet, the Chinese language uses symbols called ideograms, which represent ideas or concepts, rather than sounds. There are thousands of ideograms, and memorization is the main way to learn this written form. A person must know approximately five thousand symbols to read a newspaper.

The large number of ideograms that Chinese students must memorize has complicated China's ability to educate its population and to raise literacy rates. Chinese writing has been simplified somewhat, however. A phonetic alphabet called pinyin, which spells words with Latin letters, enables the Chinese to use typewriters and computers manufactured in nations with Latin alphabets.

Between the eighteenth and twelfth centuries B.C., members of the Shang dynasty used China's first written language to record historical events. These writings were engraved on bronze ceremonial cups and turtle shells.

These **Chinese writings** are posted on a wall of the White Horse Buddhist Temple in Luoyang, China. The ideograms run from top to bottom rather than from left to right.

Although the traditional practice of **multiple generations** living together in one home is no longer standard, Chinese families still remain close.

Family Life

The institution of family has always been important in China, where extended family—sometimes as many as five generations—traditionally shared a dwelling. Although this practice has dwindled in modern times, elderly parents may still reside with their married children.

Large families were also traditional, especially in rural China. However, after population explosions in the 1960s and the late 1970s, the Chinese government introduced a birth control program discouraging Han families from having more than one child. When the plan was implemented, families that had more than one offspring could be penalized by having their wages reduced, by being demoted at their jobs, and by facing the criticism of their neighbors. In recent years, the government has considered a more moderate approach that would reward families for having only one child instead of punishing them for having more. The birth control program has been more successful in China's cities than in the countryside. In agricultural areas, many people still believe that they must have several children to help them farm the land.

Traditional marriage practices have also changed in modern China. Arranged marriages, once standard, have become rare, although most young people are influenced by family and friends when choosing marital partners. Similarly, brides once became members of their husbands' families upon marriage, drastically reducing or even severing contact with their own families. This practice, too, has lessened in recent years. Divorce rates have risen since the mid-1900s but remain low compared to many countries.

Changing marriage customs are beginning to allow Chinese women more freedom than in the past. However, a woman's traditional role in Chinese society has been to act as caregiver and housekeeper and to follow the wishes of her father or husband. Although women have made great advances in modern China, they still have fewer opportunities than men for employment and advancement. Some common practices have even physically threatened Chinese women. The custom of footbinding, in which young girls' feet were broken and reshaped to achieve the ideal three-inch-long (7.6 cm) "lotus feet," left many Chinese women barely able to walk without support. Footbinding, which was most popular in late imperial China, was outlawed in the early 1900s.

China's birth control policy brought a new danger for the nation's girls, as Chinese culture has traditionally placed a greater value on sons than on daughters. Under the policy, the reported number of girls born fell compared to the number of boys born, suggesting that some daughters were being abandoned or even killed so that couples could try again to have a son. China's "missing girls" are still a matter of concern to groups inside and outside of the country.

◉ Health

In 1949 the PRC pledged to take care of the elderly, the sick, and the disabled. Improvements in sanitation facilities and in the availability of

BAREFOOT DOCTORS

Under Mao, China's health-care system was reformed to open free clinics in rural areas and to send "barefoot doctors" into the fields. Most of these doctors were young workers and farmers who had been trained to provide basic medical care. Funded by the government, they charged their patients little or nothing. As China shifts toward a market-based economy, the number of barefoot doctors has dwindled, and most clinics are privately owned, making health care unaffordable for many Chinese.

Traditional **Chinese medicine** uses herbs to cure sickness and alleviate pain. Hospital pharmacies continue to stock these herbal cures.

modern medical care have raised the life expectancy figure for the Chinese to 71 years, compared to 67 for Asia as a whole. The infant mortality rate in China has fallen to 31 deaths in every 1,000 live births, compared to 55 out of 1,000 in Asia as a whole. However, a relatively small number of well-trained doctors are available to treat a vast population, raising questions about the future of Chinese health care.

In addition to modern medical techniques, the Chinese practice traditional methods for curing illness. Special herbs and attention to nutrition are regarded as alternatives to modern drugs. Acupuncture, one of China's oldest forms of treatment, involves the insertion of needles at pressure points in the body to relieve pain and to cure disease. Since the 1950s, acupuncturists have used the procedure to numb patients who are about to have surgery, and the technique has gained greater acceptance outside of China as well.

China's most urgent health problem at the beginning of the twenty-first century is AIDS. Although Chinese officials had long denied a national AIDS problem, they revealed in 2001 that hundreds of thousands of citizens were already infected with HIV (the virus that causes AIDS) and that the numbers were still rising. Many of those infected are poor peasants and farmers, and some rural villages are estimated to have an infection rate of close to 80 percent. Reasons for the outbreak include unsanitary techniques for blood transfusions and other medical procedures, and a lack of education and public knowledge about how the virus is spread. As China attempts to manage the epidemic, health-care workers will need to address these issues.

Education

At the beginning of the 1900s, only 15 percent of China's population could read and write. In the last half of the twentieth century, the educational system changed radically. Primary education became available for all children, and adult education programs were aimed at increasing literacy among China's older population. By the late 1990s, more than 80 percent of Chinese adults were literate.

In the mid 1980s, a new plan to enforce nine years of compulsory education was implemented. Differences exist between rural and urban facilities, and the number of qualified teachers is too low for the number of school-aged Chinese. All the same, most Chinese children attend elementary school and at least three years of secondary school. In elementary school, they study the Chinese language, geography, history, mathematics, natural sciences, and physical education. At the secondary level, their studies may include vocational and technical courses. Foreign languages—including English—and the sciences are also an important part of the coursework.

A young scholar

University education has become a priority for China in recent times, but the number of openings is low, and the number of applicants is high. University entrance exams are difficult, and fewer than 5 percent of high school graduates get into postsecondary institutions. In addition, educational facilities have historically not kept pace with population growth. Some of the student demonstrations in the late 1980s were directed against shortages of housing and meals within the university system. As China faces the future, expanding and updating educational facilities will be critical to preparing the population for its role in the modern world.

CULTURAL LIFE

China's long history is filled with discoveries, innovations, and artistic wonders. From painting and poetry to food and film, China's cultural life displays great depth and variety. Although the country's past has also included tragedy, upheaval, and periods during which the arts have suffered, the Chinese people have persevered to produce a rich cultural tradition that continues in the twenty-first century.

▶ Literature

Perhaps the most widely read of all Chinese classical literature are the Five Classics, used by the philosopher Confucius in his teachings during the sixth century B.C. These writings include poetry, history, and philosophy and contain the key political and ethical concepts of Confucianism. Many of Confucius's own sayings, recorded by his pupils, are collected in a book called *The Analects*.

The Tang period (A.D. 618–907) was the golden age of Chinese poetry. The most distinguished writers of this period were Li Bo,

Du Fu, and Bo Juyi. They produced romantic ballads, political poetry, and satiric verse. The Ming dynasty (1368–1644) was the age of the novel. Two famous works of the time are Wu Cheng-en's *Journey to the West*, which introduced the popular character of the Monkey King, and *The Romance of the Three Kingdoms*, attributed to the writer Luo Guanzhong. This novel recounts the activities of rival warlords during the centuries that followed the fall of the Han family of rulers.

The late 1800s brought new literary themes, which described China's loss of dignity at the hands of European powers. The author Kang Youwei was active in politics and wrote about the suffering of China and the problem of inequality. One of China's greatest writers in the early twentieth century was Lu Xun. Lu wanted to reach the common people, and he chose to write in the vernacular (everyday language) rather than in scholarly Chinese. His work describes the effects of poverty, superstition, and human suffering on China.

THE MONKEY KING COMES HOME

"He was trying to find his way when he heard the call of cranes and the cry of monkeys; the call of cranes reverberated in the heavens, and the cry of monkeys moved his spirit with sadness. 'Little ones,' he called out, 'I have returned!' From the crannies of the cliff, from the flowers and the bushes, and from the wood and the trees, monkeys great and small leaped out by the tens of thousands and surrounded the Handsome Monkey King. They all kowtowed and cried, 'Great King!'"

— from *Journey to the West* by Wu Cheng-en, translated by Anthony Yu

After 1949 the PRC ordered all authors to write stories that praised the new Communist system. Writers who did not follow this guideline did not get their books published in China, and the most widely read works in the 1960s and 1970s were those of Mao Zedong. In recent decades, writers have returned to traditional Chinese styles while also exploring new literary themes and techniques. Although more freedom of expression is allowed than in the past, the Communist Party still imposes restrictions on works published in China. In 2000 the novelist and playwright Gao Xingjian, much of whose writing is banned in China, became the first Chinese author to win the Nobel Prize.

Fiction such as mysteries, action and detective stories, and romance novels are also popular in China. Urban readers can pick up paperbacks and magazines at sidewalk stalls.

◎ Performing Arts and Film

Chinese music has a long history, dating back to court musicians who played for ancient China's emperors and their guests. Traditional Chinese folk music may be played on instruments such as the *pipa* (a four-stringed, guitarlike instrument), the *zheng* (a Chinese harp, with thirteen to twenty-one strings), the *suona* (a horn), or the *dizi* (a flute). Various drums, gongs, and cymbals also appear among Chinese musical instruments. Modern Chinese musicians have adopted new styles, sometimes influenced by groups that perform in Hong Kong and Taiwan.

Music also plays a large part in traditional Chinese drama. In fact, Chinese theater is often called Chinese opera. Most of the plots are familiar to the audience and are based on historic events, religious stories, or folktales. The action is played out through songs, dialogue, and highly stylized movements and gestures that may even include acrobatics or martial arts. The actors wear elaborate makeup and costumes, but sets are usually simple.

A **Chinese opera** is performed in Beijing. For a link to a site with additional information on Chinese opera, go to vgsbooks.com.

Like many aspects of Chinese culture, the film industry, which had enjoyed moderate success since its beginnings in 1917, fared badly during the Cultural Revolution. However, it was revived in the late 1900s, especially by the efforts of a talented group of directors known as the Fifth Generation. These directors included Chen Kaige, Wu Ziniu, and Zhang Yimou, who used their work to combine the beauty of the Chinese landscape with the scope of Chinese history and culture. A thriving kung fu (martial arts) film tradition in Hong Kong has generated international stars such as Chow Yun-Fat, Jet Li, Jackie Chan, and Bruce Lee. Studios in Hong Kong and other Chinese cities continue to produce popular movies, and modern Chinese film has a wide international audience.

Visual Arts

Early Chinese watercolor paintings were done on pottery and silk. Natural images, such as landscapes, flowers, and animals, were popular during China's imperial era. Painters also depicted officials of the Chinese court, as well as the emperors themselves. An additional element in many paintings was calligraphy (elaborate hand-lettering). Popular throughout China's history, calligraphy emphasizes the beauty, precision, and intricacy of Chinese characters. Elegantly penned poems often appear alongside or on painted artworks.

Although Chinese pottery has a long tradition, the period of the Ming dynasty (1368–1644) was a time of special excellence in decorative arts. Red-and-black lacquered boxes and delicate blue-and-white ceramics became trademarks of this creative period in imperial China.

種馗利劍直堪磨 昨夜
千盅醉類酌醒目
靜心觀
宇內
斯民
再造
起沉疴
作正於丁丑年
六時臨軍兄

Contemporary watercolor **paintings** often include calligraphy to increase the dramatic effect or to tell a story.

Modern art began in China at the turn of the twentieth century, when national themes moved away from tradition and toward methods that dramatized current events. Li Hua, for example, is famous for his woodcuts, which depict the exploitation of the Chinese by foreigners.

China's Communist government adopted a political ideology for art, called Socialist Realism. Works had to be realistic in form but also had to illustrate socialist themes, such as the achievements of the people and the building of socialism. In the late 1900s, artists such as Xu Bing and Wenda Gu moved away from Socialist Realism to experiment with a variety of techniques and subjects, producing prints, sculpture, photographs, and paintings. Many contemporary artists use their work to comment on life and society in modern China, but they run the risk of the government's disapproval, and some artists choose to continue their careers in other countries.

Religion

China's Communist government discourages the practice of religion. Nevertheless, religious believers may follow their faiths as long as they do not seek to convert others. The three main religions of ancient

China were Confucianism, Buddhism, and Taoism. Over the centuries, some Chinese have combined various elements of these faiths, along with the customs of traditional folk religions.

Founded by Confucius in the sixth century B.C., Confucianism is a code of ethics rather than a set of rituals and, in some ways, is more of a philosophy than a religion. The ideals of Confucius strongly influenced Chinese society for two thousand years. Confucianism stresses harmony, tradition, and moral standards. Reverence for one's ancestors and the idea that the family is the basis of all human relationships are also key elements of Confucianism. In the area of government, Confucius taught that the role of rulers is to bring happiness to their subjects. During the Han dynasty, Confucian ideas led to the development of a state system run by people who were considered models of morality and who were promoted within the bureaucracy on the basis of merit.

Buddhism, introduced from India, is based on the teachings of Siddhartha Gautama (Buddha), a prince who lived in India in the sixth century B.C. He gave up a life of luxury to seek divine knowledge. Buddhism took root in China between A.D. 300 and A.D. 500.

Buddhist monks pray at Chuk Lam Shim Yuen (Bamboo Forest) Monastery in Hong Kong.

THE FALUN GONG

In 1999 the Chinese government banned a group called the Falun Gong. Members of the Falun Gong, including its founder Li Hongzhi, state that the group is not a religion but a movement based on meditation and the attainment of physical and spiritual health. The government, on the other hand, maintains that the group is a dangerous sect that threatens the stability of Chinese society.

Lamaism—followed by the people in Xizang—derives from Buddhism but has also adopted traditional beliefs long held by local people. During the Cultural Revolution, many monks in Xizang were arrested, and many religious buildings and objects were destroyed. Conflicts between the government and the followers of Lamaism continue, but the Tibetans have retained their religion, and it remains a unifying force in their culture.

Taoism developed in the fourth century B.C. and is based on *Dao De Jing (The Way and the Virtue)*. These writings encourage contemplation and a lifestyle that is in harmony with nature and the universe.

The Islamic religion, founded by the seventh century A.D. prophet Muhammad in what became Saudi Arabia, also has followers in China. Although government figures are scarce, estimates indicate that about 2 percent of the Chinese are Muslims. Most of the religion's members are Hui who live near Mongolian areas that have historical ties to Islamic nations farther west. A small Christian minority also exists in China.

Holidays and Festivals

Official holidays in China include National Day, celebrated on October 1 and 2. This occasion marks the anniversary of the PRC's founding and is usually celebrated with public fireworks displays and parties or parades. Children's Day falls on June 1, and Chinese children enjoy presents and parties in their honor.

Traditional festivals, many of them with Buddhist origins, are also popular throughout the country. The most important celebration of the year is the Spring Festival, or Lunar New Year. Preparations and festivities may last for weeks and include lots of decorations, food, firecrackers, and parades. The ancient Lantern Festival wraps things up on the fifteenth day of the first lunar month.

In the summer, the Dragon Boat Festival attracts hundreds of spectators to Chinese rivers and lakes, where costumed rowers race colorful boats to the rhythm of drums and gongs. The Dragon Boat Festival probably began as a tribute to the river god, but the celebration is also

In the Chang Dian Village in Beijing, dancers dress in costumes to perform **the lion dance.** Go to vgsbooks.com to find links where you can learn more about Chinese festivals, including the Chinese New Year.

in memory of Qu Yuan, a famous Chinese poet and patriot who lived more than two thousand years ago.

The Mid-Autumn Festival celebrates the harvesting of rice and wheat crops but also honors the moon, which appears fuller and brighter on this night than at any other time of the year. Not all Chinese observe the traditional ceremonies of the festival, but it is a popular time for family reunions, and most people still enjoy gathering with friends and relatives and munching on moon cakes (filled pastries) as they admire the full moon.

◉ Food

Chinese cuisine is popular throughout the world, although the Chinese eat many foods—including shark fins, bird's-nest soup, slugs, frogs, jellyfish, and seaweed—that are unfamiliar to some diners outside China. China's shortage of grazing land near populated areas and its lack of feed for livestock make meat a luxury. When meat is available, pork and fowl are far more common than lamb and beef.

The Chinese have a special way of cooking, called stir-frying, in which vegetables and meat are quickly stirred in hot oil in a round pan called a wok. The Chinese use slender wooden rods called chopsticks to eat their meals. Tasty sauces mixed with rice, noodles, and bean curd make up the balance of an ordinary Chinese meal. Common beverages are tea and beer, and diners enjoy rice wine on ceremonial occasions.

Chinese food differs from region to region. The best-known regional cuisines are from Guangdong, Sichuan, and Hunan provinces. Despite the many styles of Chinese food preparation,

SWEET AND SOUR PORK

This traditional dish is stir-fried, a technique that Chinese cooks have used for centuries.

1 pound lean pork

salt

½ egg white, lightly beaten

2 tablespoons cornstarch

5 tablespoons vegetable oil

4 slices ginger

1 medium onion, thinly sliced

1 red or green bell pepper, cut into one-inch squares

Sauce:

1 20-ounce can pineapple chunks in juice

1 tablespoon cornstarch

2 tablespoons water

3½ tablespoons rice wine vinegar

1 tablespoon light soy sauce

1½ tablespoons sugar

1 tablespoon tomato purée

1. Cut pork into 1-inch cubes. Sprinkle lightly with salt, dip in egg white, and dust with cornstarch. Set aside.
2. Drain pineapple chunks, saving 3 to 4 tablespoons of the juice. To make sauce, combine juice, 1 tablespoon cornstarch, water, rice wine vinegar, soy sauce, sugar, and tomato purée. Stir until well blended.
3. Heat oil in wok or frying pan. Add pork and stir-fry over medium heat for 3 minutes. Carefully remove pork with a slotted spoon and set aside.
4. Carefully drain away half of the oil left in the pan. Add ginger and onion and stir-fry for 1 minute. Add pineapple and bell pepper and continue to stir-fry for another minute. Pour in sauce and stir until sauce thickens. Return pork to pan and stir over medium heat for 1 to 2 minutes, or until pork is well coated with sauce. Serve with rice.

Serves 4 to 6

the diet of the average Chinese consists mainly of rice or noodles and vegetables. Estimates suggest that as many as 10 to 15 percent of the Chinese population, particularly in small towns and less industrialized areas, suffers from inadequate nutrition.

Sports and Recreation

With their origins more than one thousand years ago, the martial arts are one of the oldest forms of physical discipline in China. A complex blend of self-defense, exercise, sport, and philosophy, Chinese martial arts encompass a wide range of styles and schools. *Taijiquan,* often called tai chi, is a well-known form that has gained a growing following outside of China. Like all the martial arts, taijiquan's movements are based on ideas of combat, but Taoist theories of focusing internal energy are also central to the discipline. The form is believed to have many health benefits, and each morning large groups of people, especially the elderly, can be seen in Chinese parks and squares practicing taijiquan.

The Chinese also enjoy competitive sports including basketball and soccer, and table tennis (also called Ping-Pong) is a great favorite. Chinese Olympic athletes have traditionally excelled in events such as diving, gymnastics, and weight lifting. At the 2002 Winter Olympics, Chinese speed skaters won a total of seven medals.

AN OLD FAVORITE

Mah-jongg is a complex game of dice and tiles that has been played in China for hundreds of years. It was banned during the Cultural Revolution, both because of its connection to the past and because of its popularity as a gambling game. However, it never disappeared, and in modern times many Chinese people enjoy playing mah-jongg at home, in parks, and at teahouses.

THE ECONOMY

Since the PRC was established in 1949, it has devised and implemented a series of five-year plans focused on economic development and the modernization of agriculture. In the 1950s, the government took control of farms, industries, and businesses and allocated money and labor to construct railways and roads. New laws combined farmland into collective units called communes, and economic planning programs devoted special attention to industry.

Political upheavals after 1949 hampered economic stability in China. However, Deng Xiaoping introduced reform policies in the 1970s and 1980s that encouraged growth and modernization in agriculture and that began a gradual shift toward a more open, market-based economy.

Even after Deng's death in 1997, the reforms continued. By the end of the 1990s, these new policies had caused sweeping changes in China. Growing privatization allowed businesses and factories previously owned by the government to be purchased by private owners and

investors, many of them foreign. Private enterprise and business was increasingly legal. The state no longer controlled prices of most goods. A stock exchange opened in Shanghai, international trade increased, industrial production rose, and China's economy became one of the fastest growing in the world.

In places where new factory and service jobs opened, living standards also began to improve. A variety of foreign and domestic products became more widely available to a population that had more money to spend. At the same time, rapid growth brought inflation, as rising wages led to higher production costs and retail prices. As competition among manufacturers continues to increase, older and less efficient businesses—including many that remain state-run, such as some food factories—will be unable to compete. These enterprises may be forced to go into debt or to close down, causing unemployment. In addition, large-scale economic issues such as taxes still have to be addressed.

Agriculture

Farming is the livelihood of about 50 percent of China's people, but less than 15 percent of the nation's vast territory is under cultivation. Only a small proportion of that amount is farmed with the aid of machinery. Oxen, water buffalo, horses, donkeys, and mules are still more commonly used than tractors. Little land can be spared for the cultivation of fodder crops, so raising livestock is limited. People keep pigs and poultry, because the animals can find their own food.

The PRC's complex reforms in landownership and land use began with the establishment of agricultural cooperatives. The government pooled land and financial resources and paid wages—mostly in the form of food—to the cooperatives' members after the crops were harvested. The revenues made by the cooperatives, however, were not enough to fund large-scale farming. Under Mao's Great Leap Forward, the government combined the cooperatives into larger units, called people's communes. These groupings were then subdivided into smaller units called production teams and work brigades. By the 1980s, about half of China's people lived on communes.

When Deng Xiaoping became the leader of China, he reexamined the efficiency of the commune system and decided it needed to be updated. As a result, the government has gradually abandoned the communes in favor of a system based on greater individual economic reward. New laws allowed households and individuals to

In southeastern China, rice is harvested by hand.

farm communal land for their own needs. This change led to a period of increased production and to the development of a network of privately owned markets. However, many of China's rural workers are still subsistence farmers, raising little more than enough to feed their own households. Producing an adequate amount of food for the nation's population is an ongoing concern.

China's main farming regions are in the northeastern and southeastern parts of the nation, which are roughly divided by the Qin Mountains. Drier than the semitropical southeast, northeastern China produces most of the country's wheat. Local farmers also plant corn, cotton, and sorghum. Projects in soil conservation, flood control, and irrigation have tried to maintain and improve the northeast's ability to cultivate food crops. Yet its climate can be severe, and its short growing season hampers production levels.

FEAST OR FAMINE?

China produces a tremendous amount of food. For example, in 1998 Chinese farmers grew more than 200 million tons (181 million metric tons) of rice, and nearly 4 million tons (3.6 million metric tons) of bananas. But China also has a tremendous number of people to feed. Disastrous famines have plagued the country throughout its history, and preventing future food shortages is no small task.

In contrast, southeastern China receives plenty of rain, has a milder climate, and enjoys a longer growing season than does the north. Rice farming predominates, and farmers are able to harvest two or sometimes even three crops of rice from the same land in a year. The region also produces potatoes, cotton, and tea. China is also a substantial producer of sweet potatoes, tobacco, pears, apples, melons, carrots, and cabbages. Farmers in the Shandong Peninsula grow peanuts, and those on Hainan Island plant tropical crops, such as bananas and pineapples.

Fishers bring in a catch for sorting in the Seven Star Han village in Yunnan.

Fishing and Forestry

The coastal provinces of China support an expanding and increasingly mechanized fishing industry. Bigger boats are able to go farther out to sea for longer periods of time than in the past. Fishing is also intensive in the large deltas of the Huang, Chang, and Zhu Rivers and in the nation's streams and canals. Fishing crews catch approximately 15 million tons (13.6 million metric tons) of fish and shellfish each year.

Fish farmers raise four different kinds of carp—one of China's main sources of protein—in specially prepared ponds. Enclosed in bamboo frames, grass carp feed on grass and leaves, which float on the water. Big-headed carp and silver carp eat plankton (tiny animal and plant life contained in the water and in the silt at the bottom of ponds), and common carp feed on almost anything.

Much of China's populated and fertile land has been cleared of trees, leaving less than 15 percent of China forested. The country's remaining woodlands are concentrated in the northwest and southwest and in border areas, where there are few farms and settlements. Although in short supply, wood continues to be a valuable raw material for the construction and paper industries. The government has implemented afforestation (turning open land into forest) and reforestation programs in the hopes of maintaining resources and minimizing environmental damage.

Mining and Industry

China is rich in minerals. Abundant coal deposits, chiefly in the north and northeast, have fueled industry for decades. In the early 1960s, the Chinese discovered oil in Xinjiang and Gansu, as well as in the waters off the eastern coast. The Yungui Plateau and the Nan, Tian, and Qin Mountains hold vast reserves of lead, zinc, copper, and tungsten (a heat-resistant mineral), and miners extract gold near China's northern border.

Hunan holds the world's largest supplies of antimony—a metal that forms numerous useful alloys with other metals. Iron ore is a major mining item, and large, low-grade deposits exist in the northeast. With these reserves, the government has been able to expand the nation's iron and steel industries. By the late 1990s, China was the world's leading producer of steel, with large industrial centers in Anshan and Wuhan. Shanghai and Tianjin also dominate the industrial sector, but the government is developing new manufacturing centers.

The 1950s and 1960s saw a major effort by the PRC to build new factories around the country and to modernize existing plants. Industrial growth continued throughout the last half of the twentieth century. A jointly owned U.S.-Chinese auto plant opened in Shanghai in the mid-1980s. In the 1990s, facilities in Shenyang produced heavy machinery and track for China's railway system. Other industries make textiles, paper, cement, chemical fertilizer, and bicycles.

The silk-weaving industry in China has ancient origins as a traditional craft.

Transportation and Energy

With such a vast area to cover, railways are by far China's most important long-distance form of transportation. Rail connects all of the nation's main cities and carries freight and passengers, and more than 35,000 miles (56,326 km) of track crisscross the country.

Until World War II, China had only seven highways. The PRC built many new roads in parts of the country where no routes had previously existed. Some of these roads, such as those in Xizang and near the Indian border, were constructed for military purposes. Highways that carry trucks and buses link major cities, and unpaved roads connect many of China's villages and towns.

China's main rivers are still useful highways for both people and goods. Ocean freighters can travel up the Chang River as far as Wuhan, and from there river steamers can proceed to Chongqing. Smaller Chinese boats such as junks and sampans can navigate farther still.

Over a dozen airlines handle China's air traffic, with routes that link Chinese cities to each other and to cities around the globe. International airports in Beijing and Shanghai, along with domestic airports in other cities, carry millions of passengers and many loads of freight each year.

China Northwest is one of the many airlines serving China's airports. Beijing's Capital International Airport is the nation's busiest, with tens of thousands of passengers passing through every day.

China has abundant sources of energy in its coal deposits and oil reserves and in the hydropower potential of its rivers. There are also substantial amounts of natural gas in the Sichuan Basin. Coal-fueled plants generate most of the nation's electricity, and hydroelectric facilities—on the Huang and Han Rivers, for example—provide additional power. Many small communities have their own water-powered generators. The number of people with electricity in their homes, however, is unevenly distributed between the populous eastern and the poorer western parts of the country.

The Future

China has undergone important changes since the deaths of Mao Zedong and Deng Xiaoping, two of the nation's most influential modern leaders. Propaganda against outside ideas has given way to support of new technology and free markets. At the same time, reform and rebellion against China's own past are combined with a sense of the great value of the Chinese people's culture and experience.

Nevertheless, China faces great challenges in the coming years. Its huge population still burdens the agricultural sector, its obsolete industries face increasing competition from other Asian businesses, and its growing prosperity is bringing demands for a more open government. While China's reforms have already brought many benefits, they have also raised new concerns that the nation's government and its people are only just beginning to face in the twenty-first century.

As part of becoming a modern member of the world economy, China gained admittance to the World Trade Organization (WTO) in December of 2001. The WTO manages, monitors, and negotiates trade among nations. Being a member of the WTO will allow China smoother, more open, and more stable international commerce.

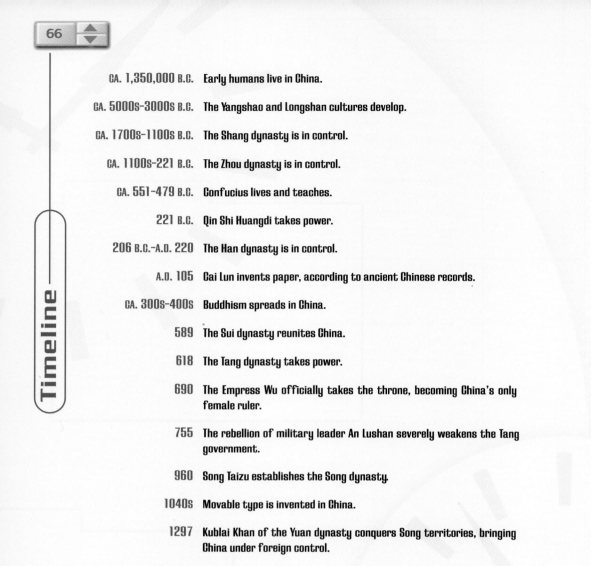

Timeline

CA. 1,350,000 B.C.	Early humans live in China.
CA. 5000s–3000s B.C.	The Yangshao and Longshan cultures develop.
CA. 1700s–1100s B.C.	The Shang dynasty is in control.
CA. 1100s–221 B.C.	The Zhou dynasty is in control.
CA. 551–479 B.C.	Confucius lives and teaches.
221 B.C.	Qin Shi Huangdi takes power.
206 B.C.–A.D. 220	The Han dynasty is in control.
A.D. 105	Cai Lun invents paper, according to ancient Chinese records.
CA. 300s–400s	Buddhism spreads in China.
589	The Sui dynasty reunites China.
618	The Tang dynasty takes power.
690	The Empress Wu officially takes the throne, becoming China's only female ruler.
755	The rebellion of military leader An Lushan severely weakens the Tang government.
960	Song Taizu establishes the Song dynasty.
1040s	Movable type is invented in China.
1297	Kublai Khan of the Yuan dynasty conquers Song territories, bringing China under foreign control.
1368	The Ming dynasty begins.
1406–1420	Most of the Forbidden City is built in Beijing.
1500s	Large numbers of foreign merchants arrive in China.
1601–1610	The missionary Matteo Ricci lives in Beijing.
1644	Manchu rulers take power and establish the Qing dynasty.
1793	British representative Lord George Macartney attempts to establish a British embassy in Beijing.
1839–1842	Opium War
1851–1864	Taiping Rebellion
1887	Severe flooding of the Huang River leaves millions dead or homeless.

1894-1895	First Chinese-Japanese War
1900	Boxer Uprising
1905	Sun Zhongshan founds the Revolutionary Alliance.
1911-1912	The Qing dynasty is overthrown by rebellion, and the Republic of China is founded.
1914-1918	World War I
1919	May Fourth Movement
1921	The Chinese Communist Party is formed.
1934-1935	Red Army's Long March
1937	The second Chinese-Japanese War begins.
1939-1945	World War II
1949	The Communist forces win the civil war. Mao Zedong establishes the People's Republic of China.
1950-1953	China and the Soviet Union join forces in the Korean War, sending aid, weapons, and soldiers to the Communist North Koreans.
1957	Tsung-Dao Lee and Chen Ning Yang win the Nobel Prize for work in theoretical physics.
1958	The Great Leap Forward is introduced.
1966	The Great Proletarian Cultural Revolution begins.
1976	Zhou Enlai dies in January. Mao Zedong dies in September.
1989	Tiananmen Square incident
1997	Deng Xiaoping dies. China regains Hong Kong.
1999	China celebrates the fiftieth anniversary of the PRC and regains control of Macao.
2000	The United States and China sign a trade agreement of "Permanent Normal Trade Relations," a step toward China's entry in the WTO.
2001	Beijing is named the site of the 2008 Summer Olympics. China is granted membership in the WTO.
2002	Dozens of Falun Gong members are arrested after staging demonstrations in Beijing.

COUNTRY NAME Zhonghua Renmin Gonghe Guo (People's Republic of China, or PRC)

AREA 3.7 million square miles (9.6 million sq. km)

MAIN LANDFORMS Himalaya Mountains, Kunlun Mountains, Tian Mountains, Pamir Mountains, Gebi (Gobi) Desert, Mu Us Desert, Taklimakan Desert, Tarim Basin, Plateau of Tibet (Plateau of Qing Zang)

HIGHEST POINT Mount Everest (29,035 ft. or 8,850 m above sea level)

LOWEST POINT Turpan Depression (465 ft. or 142 m below sea level)

MAJOR RIVERS Huang (Yellow) River, Chang (Yangzi) River, Xi River, Heilong River, Li River

ANIMALS Giant pandas, Chinese river dolphins, Yangzi alligators, Bactrian camels, antelopes, deer

CAPITAL CITY Beijing

OTHER MAJOR CITIES Shanghai, Tianjin, Chongqing, Guangzhou, Hong Kong, Nanjing, Chengdu, Harbin, Urumqi

OFFICIAL LANGUAGE Putongua (Mandarin Chinese)

MONETARY UNIT Yuan. 10 *jiao* = 1 yuan; 10 *fen* = 1 jiao.

Currency Fast Facts

CHINESE NATIONAL CURRENCY

The currency of the PRC is renminbi, or "people's currency." The basic unit is the yuan, and renminbi is issued in denominations of one, two, five, ten, fifty, and one hundred yuan; one, two, and five jiao; and one, two, and five fen. The first series of renminbi was issued by the People's Bank of China in 1948. Each series illustrated a theme, such as industry, agriculture, or ethnic minorities. The fifth series was released in 1999, along with a fifty-yuan bill celebrating the fiftieth anniversary of the PRC.

Adopted in 1949, the flag of the People's Republic of China consists of a solid red background with a large yellow star and an arc of four smaller stars in the upper left corner. The red background represents both Communism and revolution, and red is also a traditional color for Chinese festivals and celebrations. The stars have been interpreted as representing China's major ethnic groups or also as representing the PRC and China's social classes. Some people have combined the possible interpretations and see the five stars together as symbolizing the unity of the Chinese people under the PRC.

The national anthem of the People's Republic of China is "Yiyongjun Jinxingqu (March of the Volunteers)." "March of the Volunteers" was originally written in 1935, with lyrics by the poet Tian Han and music by the composer Nie Er. As the theme of a patriotic film intended to rally the Chinese people in the face of the Japanese invasion, the song became very popular and was unofficially adopted by the PRC in 1949. It became the official national anthem in 1982.

Not all English translations of "March of the Volunteers" are alike. One version follows:

Arise, ye who refuse to be slaves!
With our flesh and blood, let us build our new Great Wall!
The Chinese nation faces its greatest danger.
From each one the urgent call for action comes forth.
Arise! Arise! Arise!
Millions with but one heart,
Braving the enemy's fire,
March on!
Braving the enemy's fire,
March on! March on! March on, on!

 For a link where you can listen to China's national anthem, "March of the Volunteers," go to vgsbooks.com.

Chinese names consist of a family name and a personal name. When written in Chinese, the family name usually appears first. For example, Sun Zhongshan is from the Sun family, and his personal name is Zhongshan. Emperors and some historical figures, such as Confucius, are commonly known by a single name. The following Chinese names are written in the traditional order, with family name first.

BING XIN (1900–1999) Born in Fujian Province, Bing began writing at a young age and achieved a reputation as one of modern China's first prominent female authors. Bing traveled and studied abroad but returned to China, where she taught at universities, held government posts, and joined many associations for literature, arts, and women's interests. Her writings include stories, poems, and children's books.

CONFUCIUS (ca. 551–479 B.C.) Confucius, born near present-day Shantung, was a scholar and philosopher of ancient China. His ideas about just, fair government led him to seek office, and he gained several government posts. Conflicts with his employers and other officials often ended in his departure. Confucius had more impact as a teacher than as a politician, and he gained a following of thousands of disciples. Confucianism remains an influential system of thought in modern China.

DENG XIAOPING (1904–1997) Deng was born into a prosperous farming family in Sichuan Province. He studied in France as a young man. As a member of the Chinese Communist Party and the Red Army, he took part in the Long March and eventually gained high posts in the government. Though he fell in and out of favor with the party, Deng secured power after Mao's death and initiated significant reforms.

JIANG JIESHI (1887–1975) The son of a merchant in Zhejiang Province, Jiang pursued a military education and career. He participated in the 1911 revolution and became the leader of the Guomindang Party after Sun Zhongshan's death. Civil war between the Guomindang and the Communists forced Jiang to flee to Taiwan in 1949, where he established the Republic of China (ROC) and acted as its president until his death.

JIANG TIEFENG (b. 1938) Born in Ningbo, Jiang began drawing as a boy and studied at Beijing's well-respected Central Academy of Fine Arts. The Chinese government commissioned Jiang to create propaganda posters during the Cultural Revolution. Jiang also joined a group of artists who relocated to Yunnan province, where he developed his personal style and became known as the father of the Yunnan School. His bright, colorful work reflects the landscape and people of Yunnan.

LU XUN (1881–1936) Lu was born in Zhejiang Province. Called the father of modern Chinese literature, he chose to write in the vernacu-

Famous People

lar (everyday language) rather than in scholarly Chinese. His most famous stories are *Diary of a Madman* and *The True Story of Ah Q*. Fiercely political, Lu addressed serious social issues in his many stories, essays, and poems.

MAO ZEDONG (1893–1976) Born in Hunan Province, Mao was the son of rural workers and grew up seeing the living conditions of Chinese peasants firsthand. Inspired by the plight of the common farmer, Mao helped found the Chinese Communist Party and, in 1949, the People's Republic of China. Mao was an enormously influential and powerful figure, gaining thousands of intensely devoted followers despite the hardships caused by many of his policies. After his death, his body was embalmed and placed on view in a mausoleum in Tiananmen Square.

PUYI (1906–1967) Puyi was born in Beijing. He became China's last emperor when he was just two years old and reigned for fewer than four years. After the 1911 revolution, Puyi lived in the Forbidden City until 1924. In the 1930s, the Japanese made him the leader of a puppet government in Manchuria, and in the 1940s he was taken hostage by the Soviet Union. He was eventually sent back to China, where he was imprisoned until 1959. After his release, he was employed by the Communist government and worked as a gardener in Beijing until his death.

SUN WEN (b. 1973) Sun was born in Fujian Province. She is one of China's top women's soccer stars and one of the best players in the world. Encouraged by her father, Sun began playing soccer as a girl and has played on national Chinese teams in three Women's World Cups and three Olympic Games. In 2000 the International Federation of Football Association named her as one of the century's best players, and in 2001 she began playing in the Women's United Soccer Association league in the United States.

SUN ZHONGSHAN (1866–1925) Born near Guangzhou to a Chinese peasant family, Sun spent part of his childhood in Hawaii, returning to Asia to get his medical degree. Sun became involved in politics and founded the Revolutionary Alliance in 1905, becoming a major player in the 1911 revolution. He attempted to fuse the Guomindang and the Communist Party but died in 1925 before firmly establishing a new national government.

WANG XIZHI (303–361) Born in Shandong Province, Wang is regarded as one of the greatest calligraphers in Chinese history. Wang's best known work is the *Lanting Xu*. His characters, especially in the flowing "Walking Style," are renowned for their beauty. The emperor Taizong was such an admirer that he insisted upon being buried with some of Wang's work.

Sights to See

THE BUND, SHANGHAI Shanghai's mile-long (1.6 km) waterfront walk offers a glimpse into this port city's history of bustling trade. Stately banks, customs houses, consulates, and hotels line one side of the Bund, and the wide waters of the Huangpu River flow on the other.

THE FORBIDDEN CITY (ZIJINCHENG), BEIJING From its construction in the 1400s until the 1911 revolution, this imperial complex was only open to members of the royal court and other officials. Modern visitors are welcome to stroll the grounds and to tour the palaces, temples, and exhibition halls.

THE GREAT WALL (CHANGCHENG) This ancient marvel of engineering is a popular attraction, with several major sections left standing in northern China. The section at Badaling, near Beijing, is one of the best restored and is also the site of a museum.

LI RIVER, GUANGXI PROVINCE A journey by boat down the Li River from Guilin to Yangzhou reveals some of China's breathtaking natural scenery. Famous for its dramatic limestone peaks, the river is also lined with brilliant green fields and peaceful stands of bamboo.

THE POTALA PALACE (BUDALA GONG), LHASA Built in the 1600s, the enormous Potala Palace—with thousands of rooms—was historically the winter home of the Dalai Lama and a headquarters of Tibetan government. Cared for in modern times by Tibetan monks, parts of the palace—including tombs, chapels, and some of the living quarters—are open to visitors.

THE SILK ROAD Adventurous travelers can still follow the route of the ancient Silk Road across northwestern China. A vast landscape of mountains, sand dunes, and half-buried ruins is occasionally interrupted by still-living towns that offer colorful sights such as caves decorated with Buddhist art, open-air bazaars, and Islamic mosques.

THE SUMMER PALACE (YIHEYUAN), BEIJING The Summer Palace, one of the last residences built for a Chinese monarch, sits on Longevity Hill along the shores of Kunming Lake. The large park covering the rest of Longevity Hill is dotted with temples, halls, pagodas, and pavilions. A unique marble boat sits permanently docked offshore.

THE TERRA-COTTA WARRIORS AT XI'AN Inside the emperor Qin Shi Huangdi's burial complex, archaeologists found an army of more than six thousand life-sized terra-cotta figures guarding the emperor's tomb, complete with horses and chariots. Each soldier is unique, and historians believe that the statues may have been modeled after the emperor's own troops. Visitors to the museum in modern-day Xi'an can view the excavated pits and the restored warriors.

Buddhism: a religion founded in India by the monk Siddhartha Gautama (Buddha). Buddhism gained a following in China around the fourth and fifth centuries A.D. Some of Buddhism's ideals are the search for enlightenment, the renouncement of worldly things, and a life of virtue and wisdom.

capitalism: an economic system in which individuals control capital (money, goods, or the means of producing goods). In capitalist economies, availability and consumer demand determine the prices of goods on the market.

communes: also called people's communes, part of a system of agriculture and government created by the PRC during the Great Leap Forward. Workers farmed collectively owned land and shared the profits of their work. The PRC moved away from the communal system in the late 1900s.

Communism: a political and economic model based on the idea of common, rather than private, property. In a Communist system, the government controls capital and distributes it according to need.

Confucianism: a system of ethics based on the teachings of Confucius, who emphasized the necessity of morality and proper conduct. Confucianism also arranges society into rigid classes, an unpopular philosophy after 1949, when the government emphasized equality.

Guomindang: formed by Sun Zhongshan to establish a Chinese republic (a political system without a monarch), the Guomindang's members sought to preserve China's glory while creating a new, more democratic state

Islam: a religion founded on the Arabian Peninsula in the seventh century A.D. by the prophet Muhammad. The Five Pillars of Islam instruct followers to declare their faith, to pray, to fast, to give to the poor, and to make a pilgrimage to Mecca (the holy city of Islam) in Saudi Arabia. The holy text of Islam is the Quran.

Lamaism: a religion that combines Buddhism with Bon, the traditional Tibetan faith. The Dalai Lama, the head of the Yellow Sect of Lamaism, is viewed as both the spiritual and political leader of the Tibetan people. However, the PRC does not recognize the Dalai Lama as a legitimate political authority, and since 1959 the current Dalai Lama has run a government-in-exile in India.

Red Guards: during the Cultural Revolution, groups of high school and university students who committed themselves to upholding Mao Zedong's revolutionary ideas, which included abandoning much of Chinese tradition

socialism: a political and economic theory based on the idea of social rather than individual control of goods and production

Socialist Realism: an artistic style that first took hold in the Soviet Union in the 1930s. Beginning in the 1950s, the style was supported and enforced by the PRC. Socialist Realism was realistic (rather than abstract), and its content was intended to portray the achievements of the PRC.

Taoism: a system of thought that appeared around the fourth century B.C. A central idea of Taoism is following the Tao, or the Way, which can be defined as nature, the universe, or reality. Taoism focuses on a simple, harmonious life. Its central text, the *Dao De Jing*, was written by Laozi.

Selected Bibliography

Blunden, Caroline, and Mark Elvin. *Cultural Atlas of China.* **New York: Checkmark Books, 1998.**
This title offers a large number of maps emphasizing various time periods, combined with a text that provides an overview of Chinese history, culture, and society.

Cable News Network. *CNN.com Asia,* **2001.**
<http://www.asia.cnn.com> (November 5, 2001).
This site provides current events and breaking news about China, as well as a searchable archive of older articles.

Central Intelligence Agency. *The World Factbook 2000: China,* **2000.**
<http://www.cia.gov/cia/publications/factbook/geos/ch.html> (November 5, 2001).
This site provides a brief overview of China's geography, demographics, government, economy, communications, transportation, and international issues, complete with statistical information.

Ebrey, Patricia Buckley. *The Cambridge Illustrated History of China.* **New York: Cambridge University Press, 1996.**
This illustrated volume surveys Chinese history and includes sections focusing on art, culture, and people.

The Europa World Year Book 2000. **London: Europa Publications Limited, 2000.**
This annual publication covers China's recent history, economy, and government, as well as providing a wealth of statistics on population, employment, trade, and more. A short directory of offices and organizations is also included.

Gamer, Robert E. *Understanding Contemporary China.* **Boulder, CO: Lynne Rienner Publishers, Inc., 1999.**
This book presents a series of articles examining contemporary Chinese politics, economic issues, environment, society, and culture.

Haw, Stephen G. *A Traveller's History of China.* **New York: Interlink Books, 1998.**
This book surveys Chinese history, with an emphasis on society and culture.

Knowles, Christopher, et al. *Fodor's Exploring China.* **New York: Fodor's Travel Publications, Inc., 1997.**
This cultural travel guide includes information about China's history, religion, and minorities, as well as its sights and attractions.

New York Times Company. *The New York Times on the Web,* **2001.**
<http://www.nytimes.com> (November 5, 2001).
This site provides up-to-date news on China, along with an archive of older materials.

"PRB 2001 World Population Data Sheet." *Population Reference Bureau (PRB),* **2001.**
<http://www.prb.org> (November 5, 2001).
This annual statistics sheet provides a wealth of data on China's population, birth and death rates, fertility rate, infant mortality rate, and other useful demographic information.

Roberts, J. A. G. *A Concise History of China.* Cambridge, MA: Harvard University Press, 1999.
This title provides an overview of Chinese history, from prehistory to Deng Xiaoping.

Turner, Barry, ed. *The Statesman's Yearbook: The Politics, Cultures, and Economics of the World, 2001.* New York: Macmillan Press, 2000.
This resource provides concise information on Chinese history, climate, government, economy, and culture, including relevant statistics.

Worden, Robert L., Andrea Matles Savada, and Ronald E. Dolan, eds., Federal Research Division, Library of Congress. *China: A Country Study.* Washington, D.C.: U.S. Government Printing Office, 1988.
This title gives a moderately detailed overview of China's history, society, government, and economy. The text is also available online at <http://hdl.loc.gov/loc.gdc/cntrystd.cn>.

Further Reading and Websites

Cotterell, Arthur. *Ancient China.* **New York: Dorling Kindersley, 2000.**
This book is a richly illustrated introduction to ancient China and its artifacts, weapons, inventions, and arts.

Dramer, Kim. *Enchantment of the World: The People's Republic of China.* **Chicago: Children's Press, 1999.**
This book gives an overview of China's geography, history, and society.

DuTemple, Lesley A. *The Great Wall of China.* **Minneapolis: Lerner Publications Company, 2003.**
This title explores the building of the Great Wall and the many people involved in its long history.

Fang, Linda. *The Ch'i-lin Purse: A Collection of Ancient Chinese Stories.* **New York: Farrar Straus Giroux, 1995.**
This illustrated volume retells nine traditional Chinese tales of love, magic, and mystery.

Jiang, Ji-Li. *Red Scarf Girl: A Memoir of the Cultural Revolution.* **New York: HarperTrophy, 1997.**
This memoir tells the story of a young girl who joined Mao's Red Guards during the Cultural Revolution.

Kizilos, Peter. *Tibet: Disputed Land.* **Minneapolis: Lerner Publications Company, 2000.**
This title explores the complex history and circumstances behind the conflict between the Chinese government and the people of Tibet (Xizang).

Metil, Luana, and Jace Townsend. *The Story of Karate: From Buddhism to Bruce Lee.* **Minneapolis: Lerner Publications Company, 1995.**
This book explores the history of karate, a Chinese martial art that began hundreds of years ago and is practiced all over the world in modern times.

Patent, Dorothy Hinshaw. *The Incredible Story of China's Buried Warriors.* **New York: Benchmark Books, 2000.**
This book takes an up-close look at Qin Shi Huangdi's terra-cotta warriors and their history.

Pietrusza, David. *The Chinese Cultural Revolution.* **San Diego, CA: Lucent Books, 1997.**
This title explores the Cultural Revolution in China, including its effects on Chinese society.

Schneider, Mical. *Between the Dragon and the Eagle.* **Minneapolis: Carolrhoda Books, Inc., 1996.**
This historical novel tells a tale of early contact between China and the outside world.

Spence, Jonathan D., and Annping Chin. *The Chinese Century: A Photographic History of the Last Hundred Years.* **New York: Random House, 1996.**
This book's historical photographs and accompanying text offer a vivid depiction of modern Chinese history.

Stefoff, Rebecca. *Mao Zedong: Founder of the People's Republic of China.* **Brookfield, CT: Millbrook Press, 1996.**
This title explores the life of Mao Zedong, one of China's most powerful leaders.

Stepanchuk, Carol. *Red Eggs and Dragon Boats: Celebrating Chinese Festivals.* **Berkeley, CA: Pacific View Press, 1994.**
This colorful book introduces readers to the customs and celebrations of a variety of Chinese holidays and festivals.

Stewart, Whitney. *Deng Xiaoping: Leader in a Changing China.* **Minneapolis: Lerner Publications Company, 2001.**
This biography presents the life and career of Deng Xiaoping, the influential Chinese leader who played a critical role in modern China's economic policy.

The 14th Dalai Lama: Spiritual Leader of Tibet. **Minneapolis: Lerner Publications Company, 1996.**
This biography introduces readers to the current Dalai Lama, from his childhood to his role as the leader of the Tibetan people.

Tagliaferro, Linda. *Bruce Lee.* **Minneapolis: Lerner Publications Company, 2000.**
This biography examines the life and career of the prominent Hong Kong film star and martial artist Bruce Lee.

vgsbooks.com
Website: <http://www.vgsbooks.com>
Visit vgsbooks.com, the homepage of the Visual Geography Series®. You can get linked to all sorts of useful on-line information, including geographical, historical, demographic, cultural, and economic websites. The vgsbooks.com site is a great resource for late-breaking news and statistics.

Wang Ping. *American Visa: Short Stories.* **Minneapolis: Coffee House Press, 1994.**
This book tells the story of a young Chinese woman who has moved to the United States. Told in the first person, it describes her childhood in China and her new life in a different culture.

Yu, Ling. *Cooking the Chinese Way.* **Minneapolis: Lerner Publications Company, 2002.**
This cultural cookbook presents recipes for a variety of authentic and traditional Chinese dishes, including special foods for holidays and festivals.

Captions for photos appearing on cover and chapter openers:

Cover: The Great Wall was built about 2,500 years ago to protect China from invaders from the north.

pp. 4–5 West Lake, near Hangzhou, lies quiet and still.

pp. 8–9 Clouds hug the peaks of the Himalayas as seen from Mount Everest.

pp. 20–21 This Ming dynasty fortress still guards the western limit of the Great Wall in Gansu Province.

pp. 40–41 Schoolchildren smile for a photographer.

pp. 48–49 Costumed dancers perform at the Tang Dynasty Theater in Xi'an.

pp. 58–59 Rice fields thrive on the shores of Erhai Lake in Yunnan Province.

Photo Acknowledgments
The photographs and artwork in this book are used with the permission of:
Steve Feinstein, pp. 4-5; Galen Rowell/CORBIS, pp. 8-9; Wolfgang Kaehler, pp. 11, 20-21, 47, 55; Galyn C. Hammond, pp. 12, 14; Erwin C. "Bud" Nielson/Visuals Unlimited, p. 15; Michele Burgess, pp. 17, 19, 40-41, 42, 43, 46, 51, 58-59, 60-61, 62; North Wind Picture Archives, pp. 22, 25, 28; Courtesy of the University Museum of Philadelphia, p. 23; Courtesy of the Peabody Essex Museum, pp. 26-27; Library of Congress, pp. 29, 30; Hulton|Archive/Getty Images, p. 31; AP/Wide World Photos, pp. 33, 34, 37, 39; The White House, p. 35; Hsinhua News Agency, p. 36; Robert Fried, pp. 44, 48-49, 52, 53, 64; Karen Su/CORBIS, p. 57; Mark Anderson, p. 63; Todd Strand/Independent Picture Service, p. 68.

Front cover photo: Wolfgang Kaehler. Back cover photo: NASA.